RESERVOIR AND LAKE FLIES

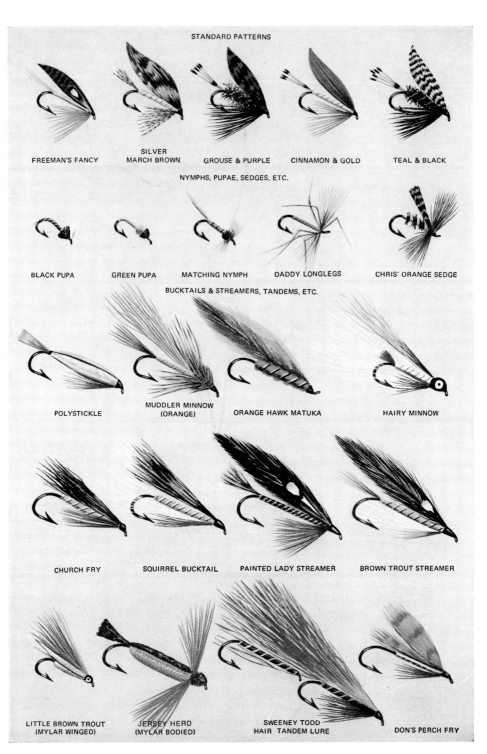

STANDARD PATTERNS

FREEMAN'S FANCY SILVER MARCH BROWN GROUSE & PURPLE CINNAMON & GOLD TEAL & BLACK

NYMPHS, PUPAE, SEDGES, ETC.

BLACK PUPA GREEN PUPA MATCHING NYMPH DADDY LONGLEGS CHRIS' ORANGE SEDGE

BUCKTAILS & STREAMERS, TANDEMS, ETC.

POLYSTICKLE MUDDLER MINNOW (ORANGE) ORANGE HAWK MATUKA HAIRY MINNOW

CHURCH FRY SQUIRREL BUCKTAIL PAINTED LADY STREAMER BROWN TROUT STREAMER

LITTLE BROWN TROUT (MYLAR WINGED) JERSEY HERD (MYLAR BODIED) SWEENEY TODD HAIR TANDEM LURE DON'S PERCH FRY

LAKE AND RESERVOIR FLIES

RESERVOIR and
LAKE FLIES

FLY DRESSINGS
AND FISHING TECHNIQUES

John Veniard

WITH DRAWINGS BY
Donald Downs

ADAM & CHARLES BLACK
LONDON

FIRST PUBLISHED 1970
REPRINTED 1973, 1974, 1978 (WITH ADDENDA), 1979
A. AND C. BLACK (PUBLISHERS) LIMITED
35 BEDFORD ROW LONDON WCIR 4JH
© 1970, JOHN VENIARD

ISBN 0 7136 0978 8

DEDICATION

To the Contributors to this book—
without whom there would have
been no book.

PRINTED IN GREAT BRITAIN BY
REDWOOD BURN LIMITED, TROWBRIDGE AND ESHER

CONTENTS

ILLUSTRATIONS

Colour Plates

Black and White Plates

Drawings

PREFACE

By Richard Walker

THERE has never been a time when so many amateurs tied so many flies, as now. More and more, anglers tie their own flies, partly because they want to save cost, partly because they want to experiment with new dressings, and often because they find fly-tying is a fascinating pursuit, irrespective of its purpose.

More and more, too, we find professional fly-tyers who are much more than mere manufacturers. Men like Lance Nicholson, David Collyer, Geoffrey Bucknall and Thomas Clegg are highly capable and practical anglers, whose products are tested by their makers in use, and who understand clearly what is needed for successful fishing. These men are in touch with experienced amateur dressers, with the result that game fishers who have not learned to tie flies can at least keep abreast of modern progress if they know which professionals to patronise.

In this situation, John Veniard occupies a unique position. Not only is he a very able angler and a wonderful fly tyer; he is also the helper and the confidante of every other good fly-tyer in this and other countries. Few indeed are not indebted to him for his help and advice; few there are who fail to tell him about their new flies, or new methods of tying, or new materials that are of value in the art. When we have a problem, we telephone or write to John, and it is seldom that he cannot provide the answer. We read about a new and successful dressing; John, depend on it, not only knows about it too, but has already discovered from its inventor exactly what materials are used in it, and how it should be tied.

I believe this book that he has written will prove invaluable, now that still-water fly-fishing is becoming so popular and expanding so quickly. In the next decade, a great number of water supply reservoirs will be completed and stocked with trout. Since these are the only waters that in the future will be immune to pollution, back-filling and all the other evils that conspire to destroy fisheries, it is inevitable that increasing numbers of anglers will turn to them for sport, which they can offer in good measure at a price that almost everyone can afford.

To make the best of this special kind of fishing, it is necessary to keep abreast of modern thinking. It is only very recently that reservoir trout fishing has been recognised as a separate branch of angling. This recognition came with the publication of T. C. Ivens' fine book "Still-Water Fly Fishing" in 1953, since when

7

a few other books on the subject have appeared.   Books on this subject remain, however, a very small minority of all the works about trout fishing and this one of John Veniards is therefore all the more welcome, dealing as it does with fly-dressings that are not only of great value, but which are not recorded elsewhere.

In addition, John Veniard has been at considerable pains to obtain and include a list of dressings of flies that have proved successful on lakes in countries other than Britain and in particular, North America and New Zealand.   Some of these dressings, like the famous Muddler Minnow, have proved highly successful on lakes and reservoirs in this country and no doubt there are many others that will do so when tied and tried.

A particular feature of flies for still waters is that it is necessary to know not only how to dress them but how to fish them, and it is in that respect that this book will be specially useful.   When John Veniard told me that he was producing it, I was delighted and I am honoured by being asked to write this preface.

Richard Walker

INTRODUCTION

THE greatest revolution in fly fishing that has taken place during the last century has been triggered off by the opening up of the vast water conservancy schemes activated by the necessity to provide water for the rapidly growing population and industrial areas of the British Isles.

This has also been emphasised by the fact that many of these schemes have taken place in areas where hitherto the avid angler has been starved of fishing water, particularly for trout.

The government departments concerned are to be congratulated in that they looked beyond the basic necessity, i.e. more water, and visualised the vast recreational potential created by these expanses of water, some of which are placed in positions of great scenic beauty. Add to this the fact that the stocking of these waters has been carried out in a highly organised manner, utilising the experience gained in earlier schemes, and the result has been the landing of trout of whose dimensions and weight we were more often used to reading about in far more fortunate corners of the world. I refer in particular to such places as North America, New Zealand, Scandinavia etc., areas which have always been the anglers' "Mecca". The last report before going to press on this book was of a 10 lb. plus fish from Chew Valley lake which I have no fear in saying was the forerunner of the lakes and their conditions under review.

Naturally, a revolution of this kind produced many new innovations, not only in methods of fishing, but also in the types of flies used. And as the scope for fly-fishing increased, so did the numbers of fisherman who wished to avail themselves of this new "arena". Thousands of anglers who had never thought much beyond their coarse fishing venues, including the highly competitive match-fishing enthusiasts, suddenly found that on their doorstep were new attractive and exciting areas to explore. But before they could take advantage of this new "demiparadise" they had to become fly-fishermen—such are the rules laid down in these new ventures. As a consequence they brought with them a new approach to fly-fishing, linked not only with their natural desire to get away from their highly industrialised and organised commercial lives, but also with the competitive element of their previous angling activities in so far that the aim was "a bigger fish than the next chap". This resulted in experimentation in fly-fishing methods and fly dressings on a scale unequalled during the previous half of this century, and we now have the "shooting-head" fly line (adopted from North America), and a whole range of new patterns on an unprecedented scale.

That last comment is the reason for this book, and I hope that within its pages I can encompass at least some of the multitudinous and varied dressings that have been brought to my notice, not only in the range of the "attractor lures", but also the results of the painstaking work that has been carried out on the imitation of the vast numbers of natural "flies" in their varying stages of evolution. In fact one of the main sections of the collection is the work of John Henderson, and the wide scope of his range of the imitations of natural lake flies is its own recommendation.

I cannot recollect any other period in fly-fishing history when inventiveness and innovation has been on such a rapidly growing scale. In the past it was usually carried out in a much more leisurely fashion, more in keeping with the highly cautious approach to trout in streams and smaller areas of open water. Admittedly we had the larger lakes of Ireland and Scotland, but in most instances it was the natural or "wild" trout that was the quarry, not the stocked fish reared artificially and then allowed to mature in new surroundings.

It is an established fact, that lakes formed by flooding erstwhile arable land always produce specimen fish for the first years of their existence. They then tend to settle down to more natural conditions, the only artificiality being the introduction of mature stock fish to cope with the demands of the angler. As a consequence, fly designs tend to fluctuate between the more aggressive lures used when the lakes are first opened, and the more delicate representations that are necessary as the lakes continue to mature.

I have therefore collected together what in my opinion are the best of the old favourites, and most of the new ones which have stood the brief test of time since their innovation. I say "new ones" with certain personal reservations, as in my own peculiar position I have been privileged to watch history repeating itself. This is best illustrated by the popularity of the hair-winged lake flies which were invented by the American Indians and then developed by their conquerors, and the tandem types which have been established lures for sea trout and salmon, etc. in both Europe and North America for a hundred years or more.

If I were asked at this moment to designate the fly which has made the most impact during the advent of our new lakes I would say without question the "Muddler Minnow" (American origin), and the lure in the same category would be any of several tandem types such as the "Dunkeld", "Worm Fly", and "Black Lure" all of which had their origins in much earlier times.

The only really new "fly" if it can be so called, is the "Polystickle", which is the modern development of attempts to imitate a small fish. Earliest attempts followed the lines of orthodox flies and fly tying, the results being those famous stand-bys such as the "Butcher", "Alexandra", and "Teal and Silver".   The "Polystickle", however, is an attempt at exact imitation, as the coloured illustration shows, and only qualifies for the "fly" appellation in so far that it is fished in the orthodox fly-fishing method.

Earlier attempts to imitate fish fry, sticklebacks, minnows, etc. used tinsel or floss (or both) for bodies, and feathers for the tail and back.   Fin movement was achieved by hackling the front in some way or other.

Dick Walker was one of the first to realise the possibilities of using modern plastics to simulate the bodies and "moving parts" of these representations, and brought his methods to the notice of the fly-fisherman in his articles in *Trout and Salmon* magazine during the end of 1966 and beginning of 1967.   More comments and instructions on how to make the "Polystickle" will be found on page 38.

Many of the flies and lures contained in this book owe their origination to the experiments carried out by those who fished the vast lakes of North America, Canada, and New Zealand, and this is a natural course of events as we now have waters and conditions in the British Isles which in many ways simulate those of countries which hitherto were more blest than ourselves.   The fact that most of these patterns also lean towards imitation of fish rather than flies or nymphs will, I have no doubt, also not go unobserved.

All in all, the transformation of the angling scene in the British Isles has been most beneficial to everyone concerned.

Admittedly some people have shown apprehension over the amount of arable land lost under the waves, but we cannot live by bread alone.   On the credit side we have received a modern reply to our modern way of life, plus recreational facilities for those who most deserve them, not only anglers but also others who are interested in aquatic pursuits—pursuits which in almost every instance have not clashed with our own.

It is only logical that the terrific output of new patterns had to be catalogued at some time or other, and I hope that this book will in some measure be an answer to this.   I do not doubt that by the time it goes to press many more new and successful patterns will have made their debut, but the inevitability of this fact is only of secondary consideration, and I hope that the ideas contained herein will spur other dedicated anglers and fly-tyers to pit their wits against nature, and that the results of their diligence and experimentation can be included at some future date.

I would like, at this juncture to acknowledge the efforts of all those who have contributed to this comprehensive work, not only the newcomers but also those 'way back in the past who gave us such established stand-bys as the "Peter Ross", "Alexandra", "Mallard and Claret", "Grouse", and "Woodcock" patterns,

Sedge imitations and Nymph patterns. Not forgetting those pioneers of lake fishing overseas whose efforts, as I said previously, have made a valuable contribution to the range of flies we are using today.

Fortunately for the lake or reservoir fly-fisherman and fly-tyer, most of the materials he needs for his lures and nymphs etc. are quite easy to come by. This even applies to dry flies, as nearly all of these are of the Sedge and Moth variety, and there is an abundance of good quality dry-fly hackles of the sizes needed for them.

Ostrich herl and Marabou herls dyed a wide variety of colours, have become increasingly popular materials for nymph bodies, and their attributes besides ease of dyeing are durability (the quill is quite strong), ease in use, and a very life-like movement of the hairs of "herls" when under water.

Man-made materials have also been utilised considerably, and I refer in particular to the fluorescent ranges of silk and wool, and the plastics for making the "Polystickle". We can even utilise monofilament to transform our deep-sunk lures into weedless form, thus enabling greater areas to be explored. Another important addition to our range of materials is the untarnishable metallised plastic, mainly used for bodies of course, but also used for "wings" in the "Mylar" range of patterns. It has not only made possible flies and lures with bodies that will remain bright as new regardless of how much they are exposed to water and weather, it has also given as a range of bright metallic colours hitherto unobtainable even with floss silks. All with the same colour and brightness retaining attributes.

As some of these new materials require a new approach when it comes to applying them to fly-tying, the reader will find that some sections of this book have been written on an instructional basis, and this, added to most of what I have said in this introduction, gives support to my oft propounded statements to the effect that although angling is one of the most ancient of arts, there is always something new we can learn about it. This applies in particular to fly-fishing where the advantage is always with the fish, although I do not think anyone will devise a fly that is truly infallible, and I hope they never will.

John Veniard.

THE "SHOOTING-HEAD" FLY LINE

In addition to the most interesting and informative section on flies and nymphs that Richard Walker gave me for this book, was this descriptive chapter on how to make the shooting-head fly line which has come into common use on those reservoirs where distance casting is essential. It enables one to get in contact with those fish that always seem to be feeding out of reach, and if banks are particularly crowded, the fellow with the longest cast can sometimes take a fish when others do not.

Another aspect, of course, is the "fast-retrieve" style of fishing which has such good results in the early part of the season. This takes the form of casting a lure, usually of the tandem variety, as far as possible, allowing it to sink, and then retrieving the line as fast as one can or as fast as one thinks necessary for prevailing conditions. Naturally, the further one can cast, the more water one covers during the retrieve, and it is in this field that the shooting head really comes into its own.

I first had this type of line brought to my notice in the pages of that famous American Magazine *Field and Stream*, way back in the mid-1950's, and made one up for my own use, more to see the effect rather than because I needed long-distance casting. It was only a matter of time before its use for modern-style reservoir fishing became apparent, and I suppose that there can be few anglers who fish these waters who do not have one or more shooting-head lines in their kit.

Before they came into common use it was the usual practice to purchase a rod specially designed for long casting, which were also able to deal with heavy flies of the "Jersey Herd" type, and large weighted lures such as the "Black Lure", "Dunkeld", "Worm Fly", etc. Nowadays, however, if one makes one's own shooting-head line, almost any rod can be adapted to this purpose. The following passages, which I am leaving practically as Dick wrote them, explains exactly how this can be done, plus some interesting information on how to make one's leaders for attaching to these revolutionary lines. The explanatory drawings are by Don Downs.

"The simplest way of obtaining a shooting-head is to buy one of the ready-made ones. These are 30 feet shooting-heads with a built-in loop at one end, to take the monofil backing. However, I find this loop clumsy, and buying ready-made shooting heads prevents you adjusting them to suit your rod, since they are already about as short as I think it is sensible to go. For my own fishing I very much prefer to make up my own shooting-heads from ordinary double taper lines. Many retailers will now sell half a line, i.e. a 45 feet length, at half the price of a full line, so that a reservoir angler can have four different kinds of line at a cost no higher than buying two ordinary full lines. As you know, there is a considerable variety of lines with different characteristics nowadays; you can get straightforward floaters; floaters with sinking tips; so-called neutral density which are actually slow sinkers except when greased, when they float; and then the three positive sinking lines, Wet Cel 1, Wet Cel 2 and Hi-D, whose sinking rates are in that order. For reservoir fishing, all of these lines have their uses and I should feel very much handicapped unless I had at least a floater, a slow sinker, and the Hi-D which is the fastest sinker of all. The way to cut a line to suit your rod is first of all to attach the full half line, i.e. 45 feet, temporarily to some nylon backing, and then fix up the rod with this line and proceed to cast. You extend line until you feel that the amount that you are false casting with is just right for the rod, neither overloading it so that it requires a lot of effort to keep the line in the air, not underloading it so that you cannot feel the rod really bending in the hand. Having found the length that you feel you can comfortably keep in the air without excessive effort, you then cut the line at the top ring of the rod. You remove the bit that is left attached to the backing, and re-attach the backing to the line that is past the rod tip. There are several ways of doing this but the most convenient, I think, and also the most efficient, is by means of what has now come to be known as the pin knot. I am enclosing a series of sketches showing how this knot is tied, and you are more than welcome to copy these for use in your book if you wish. It helps if, when the pin has been pushed into the end of the fly line and out at the side, you heat the head of the pin with a match flame or a cigarette lighter, until the pin head is red hot. You then dip the pin in water and withdraw it. Heating the pin keeps the hole open so that the nylon can be threaded through much more easily.

This pin knot is reasonably satisfactory without any embellishment but if you want to make it go through the rings more easily, you can strip off the dressing on the backing side of the knot, leaving the braided core exposed, and then, after varnishing this braided core with some kind of flexible varnish, you can whip over it with floss or fly-tying silk, so as to make a neat taper from the last turn of the knot down to the straight part of the nylon where it emerges from the end of the fly line core. If this whipping is well soaked with successive coats of varnish, it will stand up to a lot of casting and allow a much smoother passage of the joins through the rod rings. It also helps if the knot, after being formed and pulled tight, is rolled on a hard surface underneath a flat ruler, to push its turns smoothly and snugly together.

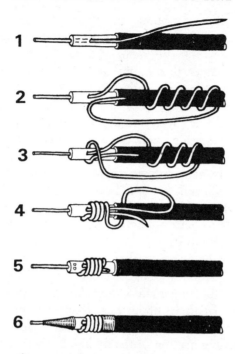

Instructions for making the "shooting-head" line.

Fig. 1.   Shows the pointed end of the nylon threaded through the pin hole.   This illustration also shows the end of the fly line with the dressing stripped off, leaving the braided core exposed.

Fig. 2.   Shows the nylon monofilament wound round the fly line, and the end brought back and laid alongside.

The turns of nylon are now unwound with the end still in position, and by turning the nylon back over itself in this manner, the end is bound as shown in Fig. 3 & 4.

Fig. 5.   The end of the nylon is now pulled so as to tighten the turns, and also where it enters the fly line so as to increase this tightness.

Fig. 6.   Shows how to whip the essential parts with fine tying silk, which should now be varnished.

I use exactly the same knot at the business end of the fly line, to which I attach permanently a piece of monofil of about 25 lbs. breaking strain and to this, the leader (cast) is in turn attached by means of a blood knot.

This results in joins to the fly line that will pass easily through the rod rings and this can be important when, as is sometimes necessary in reservoir fishing, you are using a leader which is considerably longer than the rod.

A lot of nonsense has been talked about shooting-heads recently and I want to stress that an angler is by no means confined to one size or length of shooting-head even for a particular rod.   All that matters is that the shooting-head should be such as to develop the casting power of the rod adequately.   If an angler sees reason to do so, there is nothing whatever to prevent him using a longer shooting-head made of a thinner line size.   In my own fishing, I cut most of my shooting-heads to a length of about 30 feet to 36 feet but I also keep one 42 feet long made of thinner, floating line and this I use when conditions are such that I want to put down my fly with as little disturbance as possible.   At the opposite end of the scale, if one is casting into a headwind with considerable waves breaking around one's feet, and disturbance caused by the fall of the line is of no importance at all, being microscopic compared to the natural disturbances in the area.   It is then possible to use a much shorter and heavier shooting-head with the consequent advantages of being able to drive into the wind better and to obtain a shorter back cast and thus avoid catching obstacles behind.

In practice I find that 24 feet is the absolute minimum for a shooting-head; it is almost impossible to get the line to turn over properly with anything less and even 24 feet is tricky to handle.   I always advise beginners to start off with shooting-heads 30 feet long or thereabouts and continue to use these until their double-haul casting style has developed to the stage where, if there are reasons for doing so, they can use longer and lighter shooting-heads.

There are all sorts of fallacies about this, a very common one being that the use of stiff nylon for a leader helps it to straighten.   This is just not true.   The leader is nothing but an extension of the fly line and we all know that the more supple a fly line is, the better it casts,   Exactly the same thing applies to the leader, always provided that it is so designed as to have sufficient mass.   Consequently, we now make our leaders much heavier at their thick end than used to be the case. For most reservoir fishing, I find that about a foot of nylon, permanently attached to the fly line, can be knotted to another intermediate length of the same strength i.e. about 25 lbs. breaking strain, and to that, in turn, one knots a Platil knotless taper leader tapering down to either 1X or 0X.   This knotless taper leader has to be cut at its thickest point because it is in fact a double taper and the thickest point is not, as most people believe, at the loop.   So you cut it at its thickest point and this is where you join it to the two pieces of nylon coming away from the line.

You can then either use it as it is, or knot further lengths to its thin end, coming down if you wish in steps to whatever point size and overall leader length you think appropriate to the conditions.   The additional added pieces should not, however, exceed about 24 inches to 30 inches otherwise there will be too much thin end.

If you want to make further adjustments to the leader length, the right place to do it is in the section between the thick end of the knotless taper and the short piece of nylon that you have permanently attached to your fly line.   The piece of nylon intermediate between these two can be made any length you like within reason, so if you want your leader longer it is much better to make this piece longer than to add extra thin point material.

Of course conditions determine exactly what form the leader takes and when you are casting downwind obviously you can use a longer section of thin point material than you could if you were casting right into a stiff breeze. I think failure to modify leaders to suit the conditions is one of the commonest reasons for reservoir anglers running into trouble and, often, failing to catch fish."

Best wishes,
Richard Walker.

TANDEM LURES

ALTHOUGH as I said in the introduction that tandem lures have been in use for many years, it would not be wrong to say that never have they been so universally popular as during the 60's. This popularity coincided of course with the increasing use of the large lures fished with the deep-sunk, shooting-head line. See page 13.

Tandem hook mounts fall into two categories, the solid and the flexible. The solid ones are factory-made and consist of one eyeless hook brazed onto a long-shanked eyed hook, whereas the flexible type have to be made up by joining two standard hooks together by means of gut or wire. Both types have certain drawbacks, the solid ones exerting excessive leverage when a fish is being played, and the flexible ones are only as reliable as the care put into their assembly. The solid ones present no difficulty as far as assembly is concerned, as they can be purchased ready-made, but the flexible ones usually have to be made up by the fly-tyer before he starts to turn them into a fly or lure. Before going on to the fly patterns used as tandems, the following notes on making up tandem mounts will no doubt be useful to the tyer. These notes are an extract from my book *A further Guide to Fly Dressing*, published by A. & C. Black of London.

MAKING UP TANDEM HOOK MOUNTS

MANY fly-tyers experience difficulty in making a multi-hook lure which can be relied upon.

These multi-hook lures are mostly used for sea trout fishing, but smaller types can be used in lakes and reservoirs, while larger editions are often used for salmon fishing. They consist of two or three hooks in tandem, whipped to gut or nylon, with a long over-wing, They are sometimes called "Demons" or "Terrors", and have their counterpart in the American streamer type of fly. They differ in the respect that the latter are usually tied on a single long-shanked hook.

Orthodox dressings are mostly used, two of the most popular being the "Peter Ross" and "Alexandra", although there is no limit to the variations which may be applied. An "Alexandra" would have its two or three hooks dressed with the usual flat silver body, and the long fibres of green peacock herl dressed over an under-wing of red goose or swan. Junglecock eyes and a crest over the top are optional. A further list of patterns is given at the end of this chapter.

So much for the type of fly. The difficulty which arises, is how to whip the hooks on to the gut so that they will stay put. The rear hooks are usually of the eyeless variety, but this is not essential, as the gut can be threaded through the loop of an eyed hook, so that it lies flat on the shank. It is best to start with the rear hook first.

If the hooks are whipped on tightly and evenly, there should be no trouble, but any slackness or uneven whipping can result in a lost fish.

Place the rear hook in the vice and wind the tying silk evenly from the bend to the end of the shank. The length of gut is then placed on top of the hook, and the tying silk wound in very tight, close turns back to the bend of the hook, and then back to the front end of the hook-shank again. Each turn must be very tight and close up against its neighbour. Uneven turns can result in the silk going slack. It is this tightness and uniformity which ensure that the hook will not slip. A couple of half-hitches are now made round the hook and the gut, and the silk cut off.

If it is a three-hook lure being made, the middle hook is placed in the vice, and a silk bed wound on as before. The gut is then placed on top with the rear hook to the top, and this will result in the centre hook being on top when the lure is completed, as Fig. 1. The gut is now whipped to the centre hook as before. Now make the two half-hitches and cut off the tying silk. These half-hitches are necessary, as it is very difficult to make a whip finish with the end of the gut sticking out.

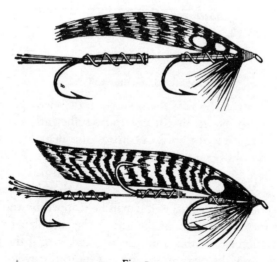

Fig. 1.

Tandem lures in two-hook and three-hook versions.

The front (eyed) hook is now put in the vice, and the procedure carried out as before. When all the hooks are tied on, their bindings must be well soaked in clear Cellire varnish, which must be allowed to dry hard before the bodies of the fly are put on.

If gut is used, this may be softened slightly in water before it is tied on, but if it is nylon, the portions which will be tied on to the hook-shank may be bitten lightly or nipped with a pair of pliers to form serrations on which the silk will grip. Twisted gut or nylon can be used to good effect, not only for extra strength, as the indentations formed by the twisting give the silk something to grip on.

Although this method may not seem to give a very robust anchorage for the hooks, it is surprising how tenacious close-whipped silk can be. Take half a dozen tight turns of silk round two closed fingers, and it will be found impossible to part them or break the silk.

Sometimes these lures are made with double hooks, particularly for salmon lures, only two doubles being used. With these it is possible to make an almost slip-proof lure. The method is as follows:

The rear double is placed in the vice and the tying silk wound up and down the hook-shank as before. One end of the length of gut is then pushed through the bends of the hook until its end reaches the end of the hook-shank. This is then fixed with a couple of turns of the tying silk. The long end is then doubled over and brought down on to the hook-shank as Fig. 2, both sections of the gut then being firmly tied in with the tying silk, which is wound down to the bend and back again. Take a half-hitch or two round gut and hook at this point and cut off

Fig. 2.

Rear hook of double hook Tandem.

the tying silk. The front hook is then placed in the vice and the free end of the gut passed through its eye so that it protrudes sufficiently for a loop to be tied in it. It is then whipped to the hook as before. Incidentally, it is most important that these double hooks have the silk bed wound on first, so that the gut is not whipped to the bare hook. The whippings are varnished as before, and a loop can be formed in the free end of the gut. It will then be observed that even if the front hook should slip during use, it will be stopped by the rear hook, which is held firmly in the doubled end of the gut. The completed mount is as Fig. 3. I think the illustration shows this quite clearly, and even if the front loop should be broken at any time, the cast can still be tied on to the eye of the front hook as normally.

The smaller lures can be tied by this method, using a small double at the rear, and a single or singles in front of it.

Another most excellent method of making tandem hooks was given to me

Fig. 3.

Using double hooks in tandem lures.

by Mr. A. K. Iles, of Fairford. The two hooks are whipped to fine trace wire, or stout nylon can be used, and the procedure is as follows:

Cut the wire (or nylon) so that it is a little more than double the length you require the tandem hooks to be. Divide the wire exactly in half by folding, and whip one half on top of the rear hook, as shown, the half being tied down being

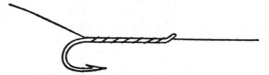

Fig. 4.

A tandem hook—Stage One.

pushed through the eye of the hook. The wire is then bound tightly to the hook, as I have described earlier in this chapter, and then varnished.

Now push the other rear end of the wire through the hook and bind this down and varnish it. We now have one hook with the two ends of wire protruding from the eye of the hook, both firmly bound down on to it. It is the binding

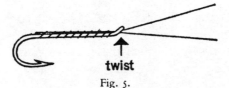

twist

Fig. 5.

A tandem hook—Stage Two.

down separately that gives the two ends of wire their immovable fixture as stage two (Fig. 5).

The front hook is now put into the vice ready for the protruding ends of wire to be bound to it. Whether the rear hook points up or down is left to the preference of the tyer, but for the purposes of this illustration the rear hook is shown in the "up" position.

The two ends of wire are now bound down on top of the front hook, but in this instance the ends are *not* pushed through the eye of the hook.

Well varnish the silk bindings once again and then cut off the surplus wire so that the two ends project about ¼-inch beyond the eye. These two ends are then doubled back over the hook and firmly bound down as per Fig. 6.

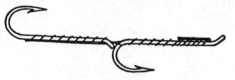

Fig. 6.

A tandem hook—Stage Three.

To make the fixture even more breakproof, each arm of the wire can be tied down separately, including the bent back end.

All the silk bindings should now be well varnished once again, building up several coats of the varnish, which should be allowed several days to harden.

Fig. 7.

Tandem hook worm fly.

then ready for tails, bodies and hackles, and in use will be found practically indestructible.

The short lengths of wire between the two hooks can be twisted together before attaching the front hook, but this is not necessary with the nylon.

SOME TANDEM HOOK PATTERNS

Badger Demon

BODIES. Flat silver tinsel.

TAIL. Rear hook only. Scarlet ibis or substitute.

HACKLE. Front hook, only, dyed bright red.

WINGS. Two badger hackles back to back, their tips reaching to the end of the tail.

HEAD. Black varnish.

Blue Terror

BODIES. Oval silver tinsel.

TAILS. (One at rear of each hook used.) Red wool or floss.

HACKLE. None.

WING. Two dyed bright blue cock hackles back to back, their tips reaching to end of rear tail.

SIDES. Strips of grey mallard flank feather—half length of hackle wing.

HEAD. Black varnish.

Crested Mallard

BODIES. Flat silver tinsel.

RIBS. Oval silver tinsel.

HACKLE. None.

TAILS. None.

WING. From brown mallard flank feather.

TOPPING. Golden pheasant crest over wing.

HEAD. Black varnish.

Dandy

BODIES. Oval silver tinsel.

HACKLE. Dyed red. (Blue as an alternative).

WING. Strips from grey mallard flank feather.

HEAD. Black varnish.

Peacock Demon

BODIES. Embossed silver tinsel.

TAIL. Rear hook only—red wool or floss.

WING. A bunch of "herls" taken from the peacock "eye" tail. (Use the herls from the actual "eye", as they are usually of good shape, tapering nicely to the tip).

HACKLE. Front hook only—dyed bright blue.

HEAD. Black varnish.

Junglecock and Silver

BODIES. Flat silver tinsel.

RIBS. Oval silver tinsel.

HACKLE. Usually none, but red, blue, black etc., can be put in if required.

WINGS. Two large junglecock feathers back to back, their tips reaching to bend of rear hook.

HEAD. Black varnish.

Mary Ann

BODIES. Flat gold tinsel.

RIBS. Oval gold tinsel.

WING. Peacock "sword" herls.

SIDES. Scarlet goose.

TOPPING. Golden pheasant crest over wing.

HACKLE. None.

HEAD. Black varnish.

Black Lure (two-hook lure)

BODIES. Black floss.

RIBS. Oval silver tinsel.

WINGS. Two black cock hackles, back to back, or splayed out in a "V".

HEAD. Black varnish.

Dunkeld

TAIL. Golden pheasant crest.

BODIES. Flat gold tinsel.

RIBS. Fine oval gold tinsel.

HACKLE. Orange.

WINGS. Long brown mallard.

CHEEKS. Small jungle cock feathers tied close to head.

THE "WEEDLESS" LAKE AND RESERVOIR FLY

No fly-fisherman has ever fished regularly without at some time or other coming up against the weed problem, and this applies in particular to the lake fisherman who at times resorts to the deep-sunk, fast-retrieve style.

Many methods of overcoming this disadvantage to fly-fishing have been introduced, but anything really effective always had the disadvantage of clumsiness. On spinning lures and plugs etc. this clumsiness is not of such great importance, yet while the fly is the most deadly of lures, none has been more difficult to adapt.

The history of fly-fishing shows a long period of slow development. Flies tied in the 18th century would be effective today. Fly floatants made in the early 1900's are still on the market. Spanish gut leaders were satisfactory. Enamelled lines worked well too. Split bamboo rods, made fifty years ago, are still used. New flies, silicone floatants, nylon leaders, vinyl coated flylines, fibreglass rods—while wonderful developments—only improved upon equipment which heretofore was sufficient.

The slow development of equipment limited fly-fishing to top of the water or a few feet below. Quality fish were taken mostly by the fly-fisher during a heavy insect hatch. Under normal feeding conditions, bigger fish were out of reach. Predominately smaller fish remained in the upper strata.

The first breakthrough came in recent years with the development of the high-density fly-line. These fast-sinking lines did more than just improve on otherwise satisfactory equipment. Entirely new waters could now be fished. The fly could be presented in deep water or on the bottom of a fast stream. New patterns and techniques proved successful. Salt-water fly-fishing expanded rapidly. Species of fresh and salt-water fishes, previously out of the anglers' reach, could now be taken regularly. As this new world of fly-fishing emerged, no other shortcoming became more obvious than the fly's snagging and foul hooking characteristics. Casting into weeds, brush or drifting near the bottom frequently ended with a high loss of flies.

It came as no surprise to experienced fishermen that quality fish were in and around these snag-infested areas. Fish spend their time where their food is. The largest part of the diet of feeding trout etc. comes from the bottom and from areas with protective cover. Shrimp, eels, fry, cray-fish, rockworms, and larvae are beneath rocks or in the sand and mud. Minnows, nymphs, and tadpoles, seek protective weedbeds, sunken brush and roots. Consistent quality fly-fishing is directly related to solving the problem of fishing these areas.

One person who has come up with an answer to the problem is Mark Kerridge of the Landmark Tackle Company, Fullerton, California, and he has marketed his idea under the name of "Brush Off" Filaments, or B.O.F. The sole agency for Great Britain was given to Veniards in 1968.

"Brush Off" is the design created by a special filament tied into the fly. It provides protection for the hook point, yet efficiently hooks the striking fish.

The teardrop shape shown in the illustrations is the most effective, and based on using this design, each diameter size of filament has its recommended hook size. It should be noted that although it is somewhat similar in appearance to our customary monofilament, the latter material does not make a satisfactory substitute. A great deal of testing went into the formulating of the size chart, for obvious reasons. Too heavy a filament would reduce the hooking capabilities of the fly or lure, and a too thin one would lose much of its effectiveness when in contact with weeds or other obstructions. It should be noticed that the same hook size may be shown on two different diameters, and these are the marginal areas where judgement is required. Either choice, however, would be effective.

The advent of the shooting-head fishing line, now so popular on reservoirs such as Grafham, creates ideal opportunities for the use of "Brush Off" tied flies. By adding the filaments to such recognised deadly lures as the "Jersey Herd", "Polystickle", Tandem "Dunkeld", "Sweney Todd", "Church Fry", whole new areas of the lakes can be searched that were hitherto inaccessible. Using these flies so adapted it is possible to drop the lure right on the bottom of the lake and to retrieve it either rapidly just above the bottom, ignoring weeds, rocks and other obstructions, or to retrieve it in short bursts allowing the lure to drop back to the bottom during the retrieve. This enables not only a greater number of fish to be covered, it also gives the angler the ability to present the lure in a much more natural manner.

Another advantage of using one's flies with the added filaments is that hook point breakages are largely eliminated when, on the back cast, the fly strikes a rock. Too often this is discovered after a good fish is lost. Half-hitches round twigs, branches, and wire fences are sharply reduced, and the long wing material on Bucktail and Streamer flies will rarely whip beneath the hook and foul the fly.

The tying instructions given here assume that the reader is already conversant with the basics of fly-tying, so these are not detailed. Only the application of the filaments is considered, and although only two examples are shown—standard hook length and long-shanked down-eye, it is of course understood that this method could be applied to every type of fly including river trout, sea trout, salmon, and even up-eyed dry-flies if one has cause to fish regularly on streams running through heavy foliage, or which have excessive weed growth at any time.

The first act is to select a filament of the correct diameter for the hook being used, and then proceed by starting with the tying silk at the tail end of the body, not the front end as is usual. Wrap the silk forward, the wrapped portion to correspond to the expected length of the fly's body. This serves as a firm basis for the filament, which is laid on top of the body as shown in Fig. 1, the forward end stopping at the same point of the tying silk or where the body will

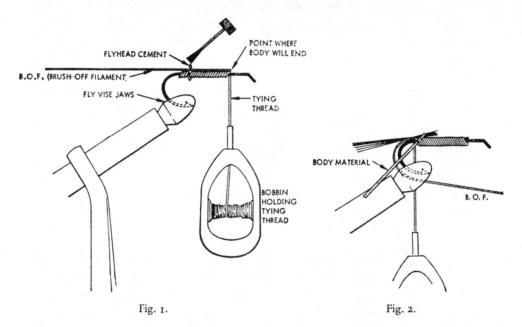

Fig. 1.   Fig. 2.

end. Hold the filament firmly in place with the thumb and forefinger, and then wrap the tying silk back to the starting point which should be where the tail is usually tied in. A firmer fixture will be obtained if the first wrappings are soaked in clear varnish. This will not only hold the filament firmly in place, it will also assure a smooth surface for any body construction which is to follow.

When secured, the filament should be in exact alignment with the top of the shank, and at this stage the remainder should be left trailing out from the rear of the hook.

The tail, if required, is now attached on top of the filament, and the body and rib constructed in the usual manner. When this stage is complete, the filament is threaded between the open jaws of the vice as shown in Fig. 2.

Now bring the filament forward underneath the shank and take two or three turns of silk round it just in front of the body as shown in Fig. 3. These turns should be held loosely in place so that the filament can be pulled into the desired "teardrop" shape. Double check to see that the filament is exactly in line beneath the shank before further wrapping.

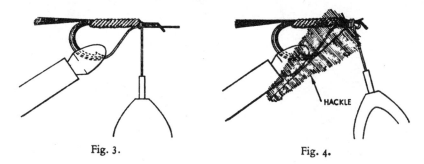

Fig. 3.   Fig. 4.

With the filament positioned in its "teardrop" shape (Fig. 4) and aligned, wrap tightly with two or three turns of thread. On hook sizes 6 and larger the eye is big enough to extend the filament through. On sizes 8 and 10 it is better not to put the filament through the eye. Whether through the eye or not, double the filament back from the bottom of the shank to the top. Secure with

DESIRABLE TEARDROP B. O. F. SHAPE
ON A TYPICAL FINISHED FLY
USING 2X LONG SHANK
Fig. 5.

two or more wraps of thread. A drop of head cement may be used. Cut off the excess filament.

On small size hooks there may not be enough clearance to double back the filament. In this case use more care in wrapping tightly and cement the end. Attach the hackle and wing and finish off in the normal manner.

Fig. 5 illustrates what a properly proportioned fly looks like with *Brush-Off* applied. The filament must be aligned with the curve, pass in front of the hook's point and close on the shank behind the hackle.

When adding the filament to long-shanked hooks, the initial instructions are the same as those shown in Fig. 1.

After attaching the tail and body material as in Fig. 2, wrap the tying silk about two-thirds up the hook's shank (one-third from hook's eye). Finish constructing the body the same two-thirds distance up the shank. At this

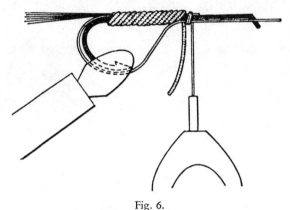

Fig. 6.

point the body is not completed, therefore the material should be held to prevent unravelling. Use hackle pliers or one turn of tying thread. Bring the filament forward and tie loosely with two or three turns of thread just in front of the

END DOUBLED BACK

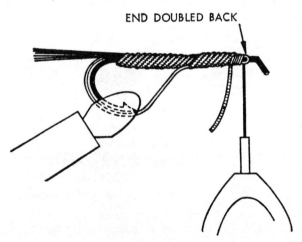

Fig. 7.

finished portion of the body. Pull the filament into the desired "teardrop" shape. Be sure the filament is squarely beneath the shank before tightly wrapping as far forward as the body is expected to go. Fig. 6.

Follow the same directions on doubling the filament back as in Fig. 4. Finish constructing the body (Fig. 7). It should be unnecessary to pass any body material

"BUTCHER" LAKE AND SEA TROUT FLY

"MALLARD AND CLARET" LAKE AND SEA TROUT FLY

inside the filament loop.   With the body finished, proceed to attach hackles and wings and finish off in normal manner.

The same "teardrop" shape is achieved on a long-shanked hook as on a short-shanked hook by closing the filament to the underside of the hook's shank the same distance from the hook's rear.

Listed below are the seven "Brush Off" Filament sizes.   Each is necessary to guarantee efficient performance on all sizes and types of hooks.   As a point of interest, at the outset it was necessary to contract and receive over 750,000 feet of filament.   This was so that the filaments could be marketed in reasonable numbers, and at a reasonable price.

ITEM NO.	HOOK SIZES
100	14 and smaller
160	14, 13, 12
200	12, 11, 10
240	10, 9, 8, 7, 6
280	8, 7, 6, 5, 4
380	4, 3, 2
460	2 and larger

"MYLAR" FLIES

THIS new material was brought to our notice by C. G. (Cliff) Joudry, of Montreal, Canada. His fishing tackle business specialises in fly-tying materials, and I would say that in this particular sphere he must be one of the best-known personalities in Canada. He has shown a great deal of originality in his fly patterns and fly-tying techniques, and much of his material has received extensive publicity though the medium of Montreal Angler & Hunters Inc. (for whom he is the leading fly-tying instructor) which is the biggest organisation of this kind in Canada.

"Mylar" is one of the new synthetic tinsels (polyester film), very much like the Lurex we have used in Great Britain for many years now, but it is much finer in texture and thinner than Lurex. Furthermore it is obtainable in embossed form, which seems to make it a much more acceptable material for fly dressing than in its flat state.

Its main use, and this is the reason I have made a special section to describe it, is as an additional wing material on streamer types of flies, and not as a body material as is customary. Illustrations of flies tied thus are shown in the coloured plate, and instructions and some of the more popular patterns are given here. I feel sure that this type of fly could make an impression on our reservoir and lake trout, and that experimentation of the possibilities of this material could produce patterns that are even more acceptable.

Another product in the Mylar range is the piping used for costumes and uniforms. It is actually a tube of braded Mylar polyester film with a silk core, and comes in either silver or gold. There are three sizes—approximately one-sixteenth, one-eighth, and three-sixteenths of an inch, suitable for all sizes of long-shanked hooks. The main use of the tubings is for the bodies of the streamer type of fly, to which it gives a scaled effect unobtainable by any other material. An added attribute is its simplicity in use, which entails no more than extracting the silk core from the tube and then sliding it over the hook-shank. Put into greater detail, this is as follows.

First tie in the tail of the fly if the dressing calls for it, then build up an under-body of floss silk, wool, or chenille according to the diameter of the tubing being used. Cut off a length of tubing of suitable length and remove one strand of the core with a pair of tweezers. The remainder of the core can then be removed quite easily. Slide the resultant shell of tubing over the eye of the hook, compress the front end of it with the thumb and forefinger and bind it down tightly with tying silk. Repeat this at the tail end with as many turns as necessary, finishing off with the whip finish. The silk bindings should be well soaked in clear varnish, and in fact the mylar body itself can be so treated for extra durability. The hackle and wings etc. are then added in the usual manner.

I am not giving any dressings of patterns using Mylar tubing, as it is obvious that any pattern calling for a full-length gold or silver body can use this interesting new material. The four illustrations show the simple process, and the "Jersey Herd" shown in the coloured plate facing page 33, shows this well-known pattern with a Mylar tube body.

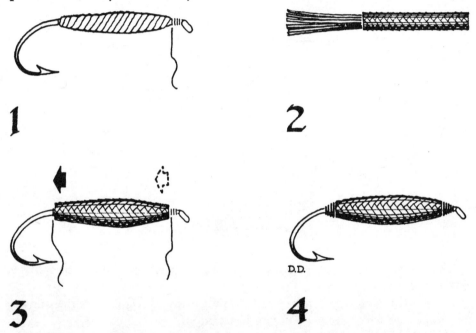

Dressing and instructions for making the Black Nosed Dace, a very well-known Marabou Streamer, using the Mylar additive as "wings" or sides.

HOOK. No. 8-10 long-shanked.

TAIL. Cream or light yellow cock hackle fibres.

BODY. White wool tapered.

HACKLE. A "false" hackle of cream or light yellow hackle fibres.

WING. A small bunch of white marabou fibres for the underpart of the wing, followed by light brown for the top half.

MYLAR SIDES. Two strips of silver Mylar, with a black edge painted along the top, as shown in the coloured illustration and page 32.

Cutting the Mylar is very simple. The material is first folded in half (it is easier to handle if re-inserted into its envelope), and then cut to the shape shown in the illustration.

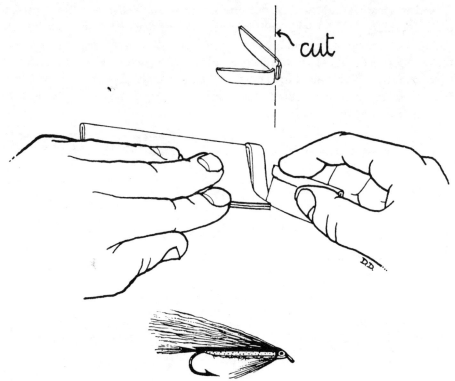

The painting of the top edge of the Mylar strip can be done with a Magic Marker pencil (felt tipped).

Head. This is enlarged with tying silk, sufficiently to accomodate the painting on of the eyes which are yellow with black pupils.

The Black Nosed Dace dressing given here was one of five originated by Mr. Bob Zwirz, of Connecticut, U.S.A., and produced in an effort to copy the five most important species of small fish in the northern states of America. Hence my suggestion that the material could be utilised in the imitation of our own species of minnows, trout fry, sticklebacks, etc. The dressings of the other four patterns are as follows:

Long Nosed Dace

    TAIL. Cream cock hackle fibres.

    BODY. Pale green wool.

    WING. Medium olive marabou fibres. These fibres should be wetted to simplify the cutting off from the stem and the application to the hook.

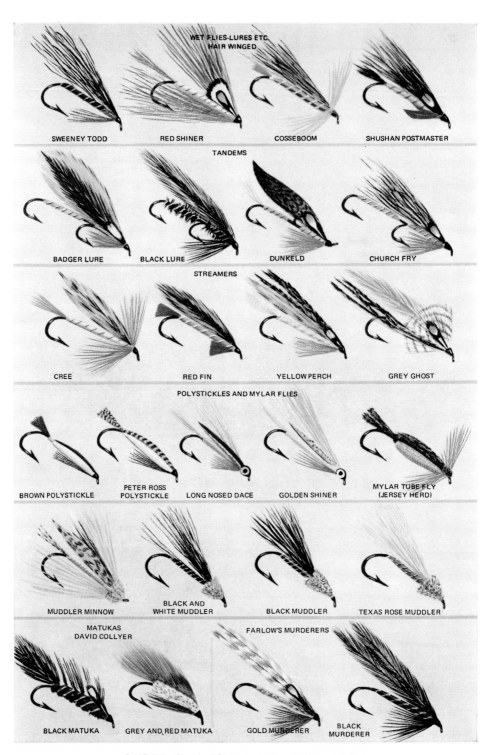

WET FLIES-LURES ETC.
HAIR WINGED

SWEENEY TODD   RED SHINER   COSSEBOOM   SHUSHAN POSTMASTER

TANDEMS

BADGER LURE   BLACK LURE   DUNKELD   CHURCH FRY

STREAMERS

CREE   RED FIN   YELLOW PERCH   GREY GHOST

POLYSTICKLES AND MYLAR FLIES

BROWN POLYSTICKLE   PETER ROSS POLYSTICKLE   LONG NOSED DACE   GOLDEN SHINER   MYLAR TUBE FLY (JERSEY HERD)

MUDDLER MINNOW   BLACK AND WHITE MUDDLER   BLACK MUDDLER   TEXAS ROSE MUDDLER

MATUKAS DAVID COLLYER   FARLOW'S MURDERERS

BLACK MATUKA   GREY AND RED MATUKA   GOLD MURDERER   BLACK MURDERER

LURES, BUCKTAILS AND STREAMERS

"FALSE" HACKLE OR "BEARD". Orange hackle fibres, short.

MYLAR. Gold with painted black edge along top.

HEAD. As for Black Nosed Dace.

Golden Shiner (illus.)

TAIL. Bright yellow hackle fibres.

BODY. Pale yellow wool.

WING. Light yellow and medium olive marabou fibres.

HACKLE OR "BEARD". Yellow and orange hackle fibres.

MYLAR. Gold.

EYES. Yellow, with black pupil.

Silver Shiner

TAIL. White and pale olive cock hackle fibres.

BODY. White wool or spun fur.

WING. White and dark olive marabou feather fibres.

HACKLE OR "BEARD". White and pale olive hackle fibres.

MYLAR. Silver.

HEAD. White eyes with black pupil.

Blueback Shiner

TAIL. White cock hackle fibres.

BODY. White wool or spun fur.

WING. White and blue (Silver doctor blue) marabou feather fibres.

HACKLE OR "BEARD". Pale cream cock hackle fibres.

MYLAR. Silver.

HEAD. White eyes with black pupil.

Little Brown Trout

Illustrated in frontispiece.

TAIL. Cream hackle fibres.

BODY. Pale yellow wool.

WING. Bottom section, yellow marabou fibres; centre section red marabou fibres; top section fibres from a large beige hen hackle.

MYLAR. Gold.

HEAD. Black, yellow eyes with black pupil.

Mylar bodied "Jersey Herd"

This is the standard "Jersey Herd" devised by Tom Ivens, the only difference being that Mylar tubing has superceded the usual copper tinsel body.

HOOK. Long shank No. 6.

BODY. Built up with silk and covered by Mylar tube.

TAIL AND BACK. Fibres of bronze peacock herl.

HACKLE. Hot orange cock hackle wound as a collar.

HEAD. Two or three turns of the peacock herl.

HOW TO DRESS THE MUDDLER MINNOW

THE American fly known as the "Muddler Minnow" achieved a remarkable list of successes in this country during the latter part of the 1967 season. I can vouch for its qualities, not only from actual use but also from the comments I have received from many anglers. The method of dressing this fly is unusual and it is apparently causing some difficulty to many amateur fly dressers. I hope these few notes will help them.

The fly was originated on the Nipigon river in Northern Ontario, by Don Gapen of the Gapen Fly Company, Anoka, Minnesota. It was an attempt to imitate the Cockatush minnow that lives in the waters of the Nipigon watershed. This is a flathead type of minnow that has its habitat under the rocks in streams.

The nickname for these minnows in Wisconsin is "muddlers". They are held in high regard by the Indians of the Nipigon area, who spear them at night with a straightened hook, or even a table fork. They use torchlight for this purpose, since the muddlers come from under the rocks only at night. I am indebted to Joseph D. Bates, Junr., author of *Streamer Fly Tying and Fishing*, for the foregoing information on this fly.

Firstly, here is the dressing as given by the originator:

HEAD. Black (red for weighted flies).

HOOK. Sizes No. 12 to No. 1 long-shanked.

TAIL. A small section of turkey wing quill (oak), slightly longer than the gape of the hook.

BODY. Flat gold tinsel.

WING. A moderately large bunch of grey squirrel tail hair, on each side of which is a fairly large section of mottled (oak) turkey wing feather tied on nearly as long as the bucktail, extending to the end of the tail and pointing upward at a 30 degree angle. (I assume that the reference to bucktail at this stage is an indication that alternative hairs can be used in the wing besides squirrel-tail hair and, in fact, subsequent dressings I have seen, quoted Impala hair and black and white bucktail fibres. In fact, in the very largest of the patterns, these longer and more robust hair fibres would be essential.—J.V.)

SHOULDERS. Natural deer body hair, spun on to surround the hook, flattened and clipped short at front and tapering longer backwards, leaving a small part as long as possible. (Use care when applying the wing to leave room at the head for the clipped deer hair part of the shoulders. This can be dressed rather heavily, perhaps using three or four spinnings of the hair.)

It is this last part of the dressing which is causing furrowed brows, the rest of it being quite straightforward streamer-fly procedure.

The use of deer hair on fishing flies is an old-established North American custom, no doubt having its origins in the lures used by the Indians. Its use as a wing material is obvious, but its qualities as a body material are not so well known. The adaptation of the hair as a body material also calls for a little-known tying technique, and this can be difficult for tyers who have not come across it before.

Most important to remember is that it is only the stiff body hairs of the deer which can be used for this purpose, the softer hairs from the tail being quite unsuitable.

The usual method is to make several "spinnings" of the hairs along the hook shank, pressing each new one close up to the last until one arrives at the position where one has a hook "palmered" completely with the deer hairs. The "hackle" is then clipped to shape the result being a very close-knit, flue-brush effect with remarkable floating qualities. This is the reason why this type of dressing is used on the bass flies popular in North America, which have to be worked continually on the surface if they are to be effective.

It is this method which is used for making the shoulders and head of the Muddler Minnow, although, of course, it is only applied at the head of the fly, not its complete length. Furthermore, it is only the front portion of the hair which is clipped short, the remaining hair at the rear forming the shoulders and some slight hackling effect underneath.

The actual method of application is quite simple, and requires very little practice. I would suggest, however, that the tyer who is not fully conversant with the technique should practice it first on a bare hook until he feels he is capable of applying it to the head of the fly in question.

The space where the hairs will be spun on should be left bare. Now cut a small bunch of fibres from the skin, keeping them as long as possible, and hold them horizontally over the hook just above where the last turn of tying silk ended. Take *two* loose turns round the fur and the hook shank, just firm enough to hold the fur on to the hook and so that the fingers holding the fur can be removed (Fig. 1). When the fingers have been removed, pull the silk tight and the fur will flare round the hook shank like a hackle (Fig. 2).

The silk should now be behind this "hackle", so still keeping it tight, pass it through the hackle to the front, and then make a half-hitch round the hook shank This half-hitch should be very tight, and is then pressed close up to the "hackle".

The procedure is now repeated with another bunch of hairs and another half-hitch as before, and is repeated further until sufficient hook shank has been covered. The result should be a shaggy flue-brush with a diameter of anything from an inch to one-and-a-half inches. (Fig. 3).

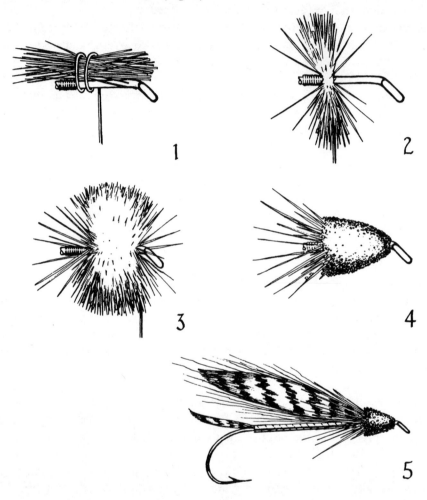

For the Muddler Minnow, we now have to clip the front part, the amount clipped, of course, depending on the size of fly being tied (Fig. 4). On Nos. 4–6 long-shanked hooks this should be at least a quarter-inch and vary according to the other sizes used (Fig. 5).

A coloured illustration of the completed fly will be found on the coloured plate facing page 33.

Like so many good fly patterns, the "Muddler" is now becoming subject to variation, and I have seen versions ranging in colour from pure white to jet black. It is quite simple to vary the pattern—one with a silver body instead of gold has proved successful, and if coloured versions are required it is only necessary to use materials of similar type to the original but of different colours.   As far as the deer body hair is concerned, as this is obtainable in several shades from white to very dark brown, dyeing presents no problem.

Other names for the fish are "Sculpin" and "Bullhead" and amongst the many variations of the fly is the one designed by David Whitlock of Bartlesville, Oklahoma, under the name of Sculpin.   He has made a much more serious attempt to capture the slim-line, flat-headed silhouette of the fish as the *trout* sees it from above, and to this purpose the hackle wings have to be tied on horizontally along the hook-shank.   The fact that one of the local names for the Muddler is "Bullhead" gives some indication of the shape one should try to achieve.   The hen pheasant feathers tied in at the front are to represent the large pectoral fins, and should be flared out for this purpose.

Sculpin Muddler

HOOK.   No. 4–8 long-shanked.

WEIGHTING (for deep sunk type).   Fine lead wire, tied in at bend and ending third distance from eye of hook.   Leave front third bare.

BODY.   Buff seal fur, tapering from bend to end of lead wire turns.

RIBS.   Medium gold oval tinsel.

WINGS.   A bunch of light-red squirrel tail fibres tied in half way along hook-shank, with Cree (Brown/Grizzle) cock hackles tied in hook-shank.

WING BASE.   Three well marked hen pheasant body feathers—the smaller fan-shaped ones with black and buff markings.   Tie one flat on top of the hook-shank over the base of the wing, and one either side, flared out to suggest the fins as described above.

Add a couple of turns of red wool over the base of these feathers, and this will not only simulate the redness of the gills, it will also hide the bulky turns of silk which have been used to tie down the body, wings and wing base.

THE POLYSTICKLE

RICHARD WALKER first put forward his theories on the imitation of small fish to be used on our larger lakes such as Chew and Grafham in an article in *Trout & Salmon* magazine in November 1966.

Basically the "flies" consisted of floss silk bodies of various colours, wound to simulate the shape of a small fish, tinsel ribbed, and backed by a strip of feather fibres—turkey or brown mallard—tied in so that a section was allowed to project from the bend of the hook and cut in the shape of a fish-tail. A wisp of red wool was tied underneath as a sort of throat hackle, and a bold head built up with turns of tying silk. The results were as per the illustration.

The first one had a white floss body and a silver rib, but variations were soon introduced—one with a yellow silk body and gold rib, another with pale green floss, silver rib, and a ginger throat hackle, and even a pink-bodied one. For muddy water a black variation was devised, all items used being black except the silver rib. Finally, in recognition of success of the better known traditional flies, Stickles using the same materials as the Dunkeld, Peter Ross, and Butcher also made their appearance.

As time passed, however, and the Stickles became increasingly popular, it became apparent that durability was not one of their best features, particularly with regard to the feather backs and even the floss bodies.

An article in *Angling Times* by Ken Sinfoil triggered off the idea of using polythene strip, and the first Stickles using this material began to appear—hence the name "Polystickle". (See p. 119).

When Richard Walker first began to use polythene for the bodies, he thought that the transparent effect was too great, but it was discovered that polythene went white when soaked in water, a most convenient coincidence.

The white floss as an under-body was retained, and the silver ribbing, and a few windings of red floss approximately a third back from the eye was added to represent the internal organs of our small fish. The result was a most realistic effect of translucence through which the silver rib and red "gut" gleamed most naturally. Furthermore, the polythene was found to be most durable, and there was no ribbing to slip or break.

The feather back and tail remained at first, but was soon replaced with another plastic—a synthetic version of raffia aptly named Raffine. This also had convenient side effects when immersed in water, where it lost its metallic appearance

TEAL, BLUE & SILVER

PETER ROSS

and became beautifully translucent, and it also bulged and improved the shape of the "fly".   Furthermore the new "fly" started to catch fish!

Fundamentally the making of the "Polystickle" now follows a set pattern, the only variations being in the colours of materials used and the methods of adorning the hook before making up the body.

HOOK.   Originally No. 6 Standard or No. 8 long-shanked. The latter is now the most popular.

BODY.   Silver tinsel wound on to the bare hook or a contrasting colour of floss silk so that a ribbed effect is achieved.   Front third to be of red floss to simulate the "gut", and fluorescent flosses have been tried with some success.

BODY COVERING.   Polythene strip (clear P.V.C.).   This has to be cut in strips from the original sheet, and if it is pulled so as to stretch it during the winding, a firm neat body will result.

BACK AND TAIL.   Raffine.   This is already in strip form like raffia so does not have to be cut.   This material should be damped and stretched before tying in, and sufficient left extending from the bend of the hook so that a shaped tail can be cut.   The raffine should be tied in before the body is wound, then brought down on top of the completed body and tied down at the head.   Most popular colours are Brown, Brown Olive, Buff, Yellow, Orange, Green and Green Olive.

THROAT.   The "hackle" can be either a slip of red wool or floss, or hackle fibres tied in underneath as a "false" hackle.

HEAD.   Built up with turns of dark tying silk and well varnished.   A small "eye" can be painted either side if so desired.

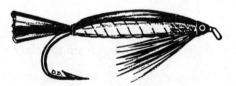

The "Polystickle".

THE "STANDARD" LAKE AND RESERVOIR PATTERNS

Although the main object of this book is to introduce anglers and fly-tyers to new patterns that have been evolved for this specialised type of fishing, it would be incomplete if it did not include a list of the tried favourites, ancient and not-so-ancient, that are still taking their quota of fish when used at appropriate times. I refer of course to the "oldies" such as the "Butcher", "Peter Ross", "Alexandra", "Invicta", "Teal and Green", etc., and in their original dressings, not variations or tandem types, and some of the not-so-old such as the "Amber Nymph", "Grenadier", "Buzzer", etc. This list must also include dry patterns such as The "Ermine Moth", "Grey Duster", "Lake Olive", and the various Sedge dressings.

DRY FLIES

Mole Fly

Although predominantly popular in Europe, particularly in France, this fly is of English origin, taking its name from the river Mole in Surrey. Very effective on slow flowing rivers, where its forward style of winging enables it to cock up very nicely. It will take fish during a hatch of Olives, Mayflies or Sedges.

HOOK. 14-16.
BODY. Dark olive tying silk.
RIBBING. Gold wire.
WINGS. Mottled hen pheasant tied forward.
HACKLE. Red/black (Furnace) wound from shoulder to tail.

Another pattern, and the one most popular in France is as follows:

HOOK. 14.
TAIL WHISKS. Coch-y-bondhu.
BODY. Mustard—yellows floss.
RIBBING. Gold wire.
WINGS. Speckled hen wing quill (as light as possible).
HACKLE. Coch-y-bondhu, ribbed down body.

This dressing makes it a very good imitation of the Oak Fly.

Coachman

This very well-known fly is thought to be the invention of a coachman to the British Royal family many years ago, although there are other versions of its origin. It can be used dry or wet, but has been found to be most successful as a dry-fly for lake fishing, particularly in the smaller sizes.

> HOOK. 16-10.
> BODY. Bronze Peacock herl.
> WINGS. White duck wing quill.
> HACKLE. Natural red cock's hackle.

When tied with wings of starling wing or grey duck wing quill, it becomes the "Lead-winged Coachman".

This fly is as popular, if not more so, in North America as it is in Great Britain, and has several variations in those parts. One of these variations is the "Royal Coachman" which differs from the original in that it has a centre section of the body composed of red floss silk, the peacock herl forming a "butt" and a "thorax"

The Americans are particularly fond of fan-winged examples of this fly, and any of the variations can be thus formed by using the round breast feathers of the Mandarin Duck as wings. An illustration of a fan-winged fly is shown in the Mayfly section.

ANTS

Flying ants do not appear very often, but when they do fish rise to them very freely. Not only trout, but practically every species. It is always very wise, therefore, to have one or two examples in one's box.

Black Ant

> HOOK. 15-16.
> BODY. Black tying silk, well waxed, and tied to the shape of an ant's body
>   Varnishing with Cellire varnish can be an improvement.
> HACKLE. Black cock.
> WINGS. Two pale blue dun cock hackle tips tied to slope backwards.

Red Ant

Tied as for the Black Ant, but with a dark orange tying silk body, and a natural red cock's hackle.

BLACK GNAT

To call this fly a gnat is a misnomer as it is a member of the Diptera family. The male is darker and slimmer than the female, and it is as well to have patterns of each as trout will often feed on one in preference to the other.

Male Black Gnat

HOOK. 15–17.
BODY. Black quill, horsehair or tying silk.
HACKLE. Black cock or starling's neck feather.
WINGS. Pale starling or two small pale blue dun hackle tips tied flat on the back.

Female Black Gnat

BODY. A strand of brown turkey tail feather, or brown quill.
HACKLE. Black cock's hackle or a starling's neck feather.
WINGS. Pale starling or two small pale blue dun cock hackle tips, tied flat on the back.

Another pattern which is as a good imitation of the Black Gnat is the "Baby Sun Fly", the dressing of which is as follows:

HOOK. 14–16.
TAIL WHISKS. Three strands from a Coch-y-bondhu cock hackle.
BODY. Hair from a rabbit's poll, using only the black and brown fibres from between the eyes and nose.
HACKLE. Short fibred Coch-y-bondhu cock hackle.

Wickham's Fancy

A first class "fancy" fly which is not designed to imitate any particular species but will be found most useful under practically any circumstances. It can be used wet or dry but is better as a floating fly, for trout, grayling, dace and chub flies. It can be even used as a sea trout fly, and I personally found a fairly large specimen most useful when the Sedge flies are "on".

HOOK. 14–16. Larger for sea trout and during the Sedge rise.
TAIL WHISKS. Red-game cock's hackle fibres, or guinea fowl dyed red-brown.
BODY. Flat gold, ribbed with fine gold wire.
HACKLE. Red-game cock's hackle.
THROAT HACKLE. One, or two, red-game cock's hackles.
WINGS. Starling wing quill—grey duck wing quill in the larger sizes.

Some anglers prefer this fly without the wings, and it becomes a hackled pattern merely by the omission of the wings.

Doctor

A fly designed to imitate beetles, which can be used throughout the season on rivers or lakes.

> HOOK. 12-14.
> BODY. Rear quarter, white rabbit fur dyed yellow, remainder black rabbit fur. It should be dressed full to represent a beetle-like body.
> TAIL WHISKS. Fibres form a large stiff Coch-y-bondhu cock's hackle.
> HACKLE. One large Coch-y-bondhu cock's hackle wound full—ten or eleven turns.

The "Devonshire Doctor", from which the above pattern was derived, is usually ribbed with flat gold tinsel and does not have the yellow rear quarter. This is also a very good wet fly.

Blagdon Green Midge

A still-water fly, hatching in June and lasting throughout the rest of the season. A good dry-fly for all pools, lakes and reservoirs.

> HOOK. 14-16.
> BODY. Emerald green wool.
> WINGS. Stiff white cock hackle wound at shoulder only.

OR:

> BODY. A strand from a swan's feather dyed emerald green.
> HACKLE. A plymouth rock (grizzle) cock's hackle wound from tail to shoulder, cut to shorten the fibres.
> WINGS. Two light grey cock hackle points.

Blagdon Olive Midge

Another fine dry-fly for lake fishing.

> HOOK. 14-16.
> BODY. Natural heron's herl.
> HACKLE. Stiff olive cock's hackle at shoulder only.
> WINGS. Two blue dun cock hackle points.

Grey Duster

One of the best all-round dry-flies, which will take fish throughout the season, being particularly good during the Mayfly hatch.

> HOOK. 12-14, larger for Mayflies and lake fishing.
> TYING SILK. Brown.

BODY. Dubbing of light rabbit's fur mixed with a small amount of the blue under-fur.

HACKLE. Stiff badger cock's hackle with a good dark centre.

TAIL WHISKS. Can be added on smaller patterns if the "Duster" is used during a hatch of olives.

Lake Olive

This is the dressing of this fly invented by Mr. J. R. Harris the well-known Irish entomologist, and recommended by Colonel Joscelyn Lane in *Lake and Loch fishing*.

HOOK. 12-13.

WINGS. Dark starling tied forward.

BODY. Pale blue heron herl dyed brown olive.

RIBBING. Gold wire.

HACKLE. Green olive cock's hackle.

TAIL. Fibres from a brown olive cock's hackle.

During the autumn the hackle should be brown olive, and the body swan herl dyed brown olive.

The nymph dressing of this fly is given on page 63.

Cinnamon Sedge (1)

I have chosen this pattern as it illustrates the rather unique method of dressing recommended by Colonel Joscelyn Lane, and I can vouch for its floating capabilities from experience.

HOOK. 5.

TYING SILK. Golden olive.

TAIL. Pale ginger cock hackle fibres.

BODY. Ginger cock's hackle.

WINGS. Pale ginger cock hackle fibres.

THORAX. Ginger cock's hackle.

LEG HACKLE. Ginger cock.

The full tying method is graphically described in *Lake and Loch fishing* by Colonel Lane, but I trust the brief description given here will suffice.

TAIL. A thick bunch of cock hackle fibres.

BODY. A long hackle wound close and then clipped close on top, and trimmed underneath and each side to a length equivalent to the gape of the hook. Taking up the tail half of the body.

WINGS.   A bunch of fibres tied in as was the tail, the broader the better. There should be no daylight between wing, body and tail.

THORAX.   Tied in and treated as was the body, the whole fly now trimmed to a conical shape.   Room should be left for the front hackle.

LEG HACKLE.   Four or five turns of a short fibred hackle.

Cinnamon Sedge (2)

BODY.   Light olive quill.

BODY HACKLE.   Light olive.

WINGS.   Light brown hen wing quill.   Lightly speckled if available.

FRONT HACKLE.   Natural light red cock's hackle.

Cinnamon Sedge (3)

BODY.   Fibre from a cinnamon turkey tail.

RIBBING.   Gold wire.

BODY HACKLE.   Dark ginger.

WINGS.   Brown hen wing quill.

FRONT HACKLE.   Dark ginger.

See also the "Grannom" which is a good imitation of a smaller sedge fly.

Ermine Moth

A good imitation of the light coloured moth, as are the "Grey Duster" given on page 43, and "Feather Duster" given here also.

HOOK.   No. 14–12.

TAG.   A loop of orange wool tied in flat and then cut to form a fork about a $\frac{1}{4}$-inch long.

BODY.   White rabbit fur.

RIBBING.   Coarse black thread.

HACKLE.   Two large grey speckled partridge feathers.

Feather Duster

BODY.   Light grey seal's fur mixed with blue rabbit fur.

HACKLE.   Blue dun.

Both body and hackle should be dressed full.

White Moth

HOOK. 10–14.
BODY. White wool rather thick
RIBBING. Silver wire.
HACKLE. White cock from shoulder to tail.
WINGS. From a light coloured owl's wing.

WET FLIES

Teal and Green

The "Teal" series are standard wet fly patterns for both sea trout and lake trout flies. This fly, the "Teal Blue and Silver", and the "Peter Ross" (described on page 47), are the best known of the series.

HOOK. No. 8–14.
TAIL. Two or three golden pheasant tippet fibres.
BODY. Green seal's fur.
RIBBING. Oval silver tinsel, or fine flat silver tinsel on the smaller patterns.
WINGS. Teal breast or flank feathers. (Flank feathers are larger.)
HACKLE. Natural light red, or dyed green.

There are many colour combinations for this series of flies, achieved by varying the colour of the body fur and the hackle i.e. "Teal and Black" would be the same dressing as above, but with black seal's fur and a black hackle.

Teal Blue and Silver

HOOK. No. 8–14.
TAIL. Fibres of golden pheasant tippet.
BODY. Flat silver tinsel.
RIBBING. Oval silver tinsel, or silver wire.
HACKLE. Bright blue.
WINGS. Teal breast or flank feathers.

Teal and Mixed

HOOK. No. 8–14.
TAIL. Fibres of golden pheasant tippet.
BODY. One third each of yellow, red and blue seal's fur.
RIBBING. This is optional, but can be of either silver or gold tinsel.
HACKLE. Black cock or hen.
WINGS. Teal breast or flank.

The colour combinations for the "mixed" flies can of course be varied, the rule being to have the darkest one at the front and the lightest at the tail end.

Butcher

With the "Peter Ross" and "Alexandra", this is undoubtedly one of the most well-known flies in the world.   It is deadly, particularly early in the season, for lake, river and sea trout.

> HOOK.   No. 10–14.
> TAIL.   Red Ibis or substitute.
> BODY.   Flat silver.
> HACKLE.   Black cock or hen's hackle.
> WINGS.   From the blue-black section of a feather from a mallard drake's wing.

This fly is sometimes referred to as the "Silver Butcher" to distinguish it from the "Gold Butcher" which obviously has a gold tinsel body and rib, and the "Bloody Butcher" which differs only in the fact that it has a dyed red hackle instead of a black.

Another lesser known variation, very popular in Scotland for loch fishing, is the "Kingfisher Butcher".

> WINGS.   Slate coloured, from the primary wing feathers of the mallard or coot.   (Sometimes dressed with the blue-black wing instead).
> HACKLE.   Orange cock or hen's.
> TAIL.   Two or three fibres from the wing of the kingfisher.
> BODY.   Flat gold tinsel.
> RIBBING.   Oval gold.

Peter Ross

Undoubtedly the most popular pattern for wet fly fishing ever invented. Its originator was Peter Ross of Killin, Perthshire, and although he only produced it as a variation of the "Teal and Red", the slight variation turned a good fly into one of the most killing patterns known to anglers.   Its main reputation is as lake fly, but is reckoned by many to be equally good for sea trout.

> HOOK.   No. 8–14.
> TAIL.   Fibres from a golden pheasant tippet feather.
> BODY.   In two halves, the tail half of flat silver tinsel, and the front half of dyed red seal's fur.

RIBBING.   Oval silver over both halves.
HACKLE.   Black cock or hen's.
WINGS.   From the breast or flank feather of a teal.

Peter Ross.

Black Pennell

The "Pennell" series were the invention of H. Cholmondely Pennell, English poet, sportsman and author, who also had much to do with the evolution of our present day hook styles.

These flies should be dressed with the hackle rather longer than is usual, and the number of turns kept to a minimum.   Pennell himself recommended three patterns besides the Black; Brown, Yellow and Green.

HOOK.   No. 10–13.
TAG.   Fine silver tinsel.
TAIL.   Tippet fibres, to which are sometimes added a small golden pheasant crest feather.
BODY.   Very thin, of black floss silk.
RIBBING.   Oval silver—fine.
HACKLE.   Black cock, long in fibre and dressed sparsely.

For the other patterns it is merely neccessary to alter the colour of the body silk and hackle, natural light red game hackles sometimes being preferred for the yellow and green patterns.

The "Pennell's" are primarily lake and sea trout flies, and dressed much heavier in the hackle are very much in demand for "dapping".

Silver Doctor

This is the trout version of the popular salmon fly of the same name, dressed much simpler of course.   Ideal for lake and sea trout when big fish are expected.

HOOK.   No. 10–6.
TAIL.   Fibres of golden pheasant tippet.

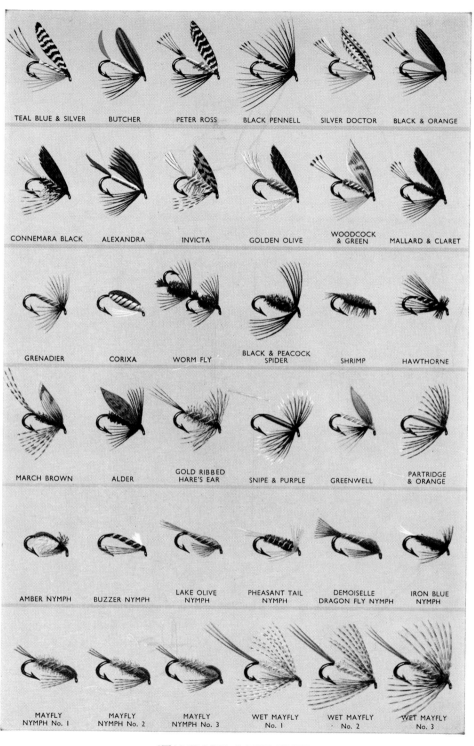

TEAL BLUE & SILVER · BUTCHER · PETER ROSS · BLACK PENNELL · SILVER DOCTOR · BLACK & ORANGE

CONNEMARA BLACK · ALEXANDRA · INVICTA · GOLDEN OLIVE · WOODCOCK & GREEN · MALLARD & CLARET

GRENADIER · CORIXA · WORM FLY · BLACK & PEACOCK SPIDER · SHRIMP · HAWTHORNE

MARCH BROWN · ALDER · GOLD RIBBED HARE'S EAR · SNIPE & PURPLE · GREENWELL · PARTRIDGE & ORANGE

AMBER NYMPH · BUZZER NYMPH · LAKE OLIVE NYMPH · PHEASANT TAIL NYMPH · DEMOISELLE DRAGON FLY NYMPH · IRON BLUE NYMPH

MAYFLY NYMPH No. 1 · MAYFLY NYMPH No. 2 · MAYFLY NYMPH No. 3 · WET MAYFLY No. 1 · WET MAYFLY No. 2 · WET MAYFLY No. 3

STANDARD LAKE FLIES
TIED BY JOHN VENIARD

BODY.   Flat silver tinsel.

RIBBING.   Oval silver.

HACKLE.   Bright blue.

WINGS.   Strips of goose or white duck wing feathers, dyed green, yellow and red, with a strip of mallard's grey breast or flank feather each side.

A small golden pheasant crest feather is sometimes added to the tippet fibres of the tail, and in larger patterns a few fibres of speckled guinea fowl neck feathers are added in front of the blue hackle.

Connemara Black

Although, as its name denotes, originally an Irish lake and sea trout pattern, it has proved a successful fly in every part of the British Isles.

HOOK.   No. 12-8.

TAIL.   Small golden pheasant crest feather.

BODY.   Black seal's fur.

RIBBING.   Fine oval silver tinsel.

HACKLE.   Black cock's hackle, with the blue feather from a Jay's wing in the front. On larger patterns, the black hackle is wound from tail to shoulder.

WINGS.   Bronze mallard flank.

RIBBING.   Fine oval silver (optional).

HACKLE.   Black hen's.

Dunkeld

This is the trout fly version of the famous salmon fly of the same name, and it has had a very large measure of success during the last few years, particularly in the reservoir type of lake such as Chew, Blagdon, Weir Wood and Grafham.

HOOK.   No. 12-8 (or larger for sea trout).

TAIL.   Golden pheasant crest.

BODY.   Flat gold tinsel.

RIBBING.   Gold wire or oval gold tinsel.

HACKLE.   Dyed orange (wound from shoulder to tail on larger patterns).

WINGS.   Brown (bronze) mallard.

"EYES".   Two small jungle cock feathers tied close to head.

Alexandra

A fly that needs little or no introduction, being one of the most well-known lake and sea trout patterns. Lauded by some and condemned by others, I personally have found it a real "killer" in lakes stocked with Rainbow trout, particularly the "Jungle" version.

HOOK. No. 10–12.

TAIL. Red Ibis, to which is sometimes added a strand or two of green peacock herl.

BODY. Flat silver tinsel.

RIB. Fine oval silver (Optional).

HACKLE. Black hen's.

WINGS. Strands of green herl from the "sword" tail of the peacock, usually with a thin strip of ibis each side.

The "Jungle Alexandra" is exactly the same, but instead of sides of ibis these are replaced with small jungle cock feathers. Tied in "short".

Invicta

Always a very popular fly for lakes, this famous pattern is now having a run of success on the large reservoirs that have come into being since the Second World War. This, I think, is mainly due to the large hatches of sedge to be found on them, of which the "Invicta" is a fine imitator for wet-fly fishing. When used for this purpose, good results can be expected right through the season.

HOOK. 10–14.

TAIL. Golden pheasant crest feather.

BODY. Seal's fur dyed yellow.

RIBBING. Oval or round gold tinsel.

BODY HACKLE. Red game from shoulder to tail.

FRONT HACKLE. Blue jay, from the wing.

WINGS. From a hen pheasant's centre tail.

A variation designed by the late Mr. John Eastwood for sea trout, is tied as follows:

HOOK. 7–10.

TAIL. Golden pheasant crest feather.

BODY. Flat silver tinsel.

HACKLE. Blue jay wing feather, rather long in fibre.

WINGS. From a hen pheasant's centre tail.

Golden Olive

A very old and famous sea trout fly, and also regarded very highly as a good imitation of the lake olive when tied on the smaller sizes of hook.

HOOK. 10–12.

TAG. Orange floss.

TAIL. A golden pheasant crest feather.
BODY. Rich golden olive seal's fur.
RIBBING. Oval gold tinsel.
HACKLE. Golden olive cock or hen's.
WINGS. Golden pheasant tippet fibres with strips of brown (bronze) mallard over.

Woodcock and Yellow

The "Woodcock" series resemble the "Teal", "Mallard", and "Grouse" series in that they are standard patterns for lake and sea trout fishing. The "Woodcock and Yellow" is particularly successful as a lake or reservoir fly, as a sedge imitation.

HOOK. 8–14.
TAIL. A few fibres of golden pheasant tippet.
BODY. Yellow seal's fur.
RIBBING. Oval silver.
HACKLE. Natural medium red, or a yellow one the same colour as the body.
WINGS. From the wing feather of a woodcock.

Woodcock and Green

BODY. Seal's fur dyed green.
HACKLE. Natural ginger, or one dyed the same colour as the body.
WINGS AND TAIL. As for "Woodcock and Yellow".

Woodcock and Red

BODY. Dyed red seal's fur.
HACKLE. Natural dark red, or one dyed the same colour as the body.
WINGS AND TAIL. As for "Woodcock and Green".

Woodcock and Hare's Ear

TAG. Flat gold tinsel.
TAIL. Two fibres of brown mallard.
BODY. Dark fur from the hare's ear.
HACKLE. Longer fibres of hare's flax picked out to form hackle.
WINGS. Woodcock wing feather.
RIBBING Is optional for this fly, but fine flat gold tinsel is recommended for keeping the body in place.

Grouse Series

By substituting grouse tail feathers for woodcock wing quills, this entire series may be converted to the "Grouse" series, i.e. "Grouse and Green", "Grouse and Yellow", etc. The "Grouse and Purple" has been particularly successful in Scotland, both for loch and river trouting.

Mallard and Claret

The best known of the "Mallard" series of lake and sea-trout flies, and probably the most successful pattern ever invented for wet-fly fishing. Its reputation is high in every part of the British Isles, both for lake and sea trout fishing. Tied in the smallest sizes it can be also used for nymph fishing for brown trout. In fact the best all-rounder one is likely to find.

There are several patterns in the "Mallard" series, but it is the "Claret" which reigns supreme.

HOOK. 10–14. (Up to size 8 for sea trout.)
TAIL. Golden pheasant tippet fibres.
BODY. Claret seal's fur.
RIBBING. Oval gold tinsel. (Fine gold wire in very small sizes.)
HACKLE. Natural red cock's, or one dyed the same colour as the body.
WINGS. Bronze speckled feathers from the mallard shoulder, usually referred to as "Bronze Mallard".

The "Mallard and Mixed" is another good lake pattern, and is tied as follows:

TAIL. Tippet fibres.
BODY. In three equal sections of orange, red and fiery brown seal's fur, tied in from the tail in that order.
RIBBING. Oval gold tinsel.
HACKLE. Natural dark red cock or hen's.
WINGS. Bronze mallard.

Mallard and Green

Tied as for the "Mallard and Claret" but with a body of green seal's fur, a silver rib, and a natural light red or dyed green hackle.

Mallard and Silver

Tied as for "Mallard and Claret" but with a silver tinsel body.

Freeman's Fancy

A lesser known but none the less very effective fly for lake fishing, which also uses the bronze mallard feather for its wings.

HOOK. No. 12–10, and up to size 8 if used for sea trout fishing.

TAIL. A bunch of orange toucan breast feathers, or substitute. (A small golden pheasant crest is good.)

BODY. Flat gold tinsel.

WINGS. Bronze mallard, with a very small jungle cock feather each side.

HACKLE. Dyed bright magenta.

Grenadier

This pattern is one of several described by Col. Esmond Drury in an article in the *Fishing Gazette* of April 1958. They were designed by Dr. Bell of Wrington particularly for the lakes and reservoirs of Chew Valley and Blagdon. The other patterns are the "Large Amber Nymph", "Small Amber Nymph", "Buzzer Nymph" and "Corixa", and the dressings of all these are included in this book. See Index.

HOOK. No. 13.

BODY. Hot orange floss or seal's fur.

RIBBING. Oval gold tinsel.

HACKLE. Two turns of ginger or light furnace cock.

Corixa

One of the patterns mentioned above, the dressing being as follows:

HOOK. No. 12 or 13.

BODY. White or cream floss silk dressed very fat.

RIBBING. Beige or brown silk.

WING CASE. A strip of woodcock wing fibres tied in at the tail, brought over to lay on top of the body and tied in at the head.

LEGS. A few fibres of white or cream hen's hackle tied in under the head.

Note. If the hook is first painted white, it will prevent the white floss body becoming dull when wet.

Worm Fly

This is another pattern which has come very much to the fore with the advent of reservoir fishing, and is another of the flies mentioned in Col. Esmond Drury's list of patterns. It is best described as two "Red Tag" flies in tandem.

HOOKS. Two tied in tandem—No. 12 or 13.

(Tail Fly)

TAG. Red floss silk.

BODY. Bronze peacock herl, with a small tip of flat gold tinsel wound under the tail (optional).

HACKLE. Dark red cock or hen.

(Front Fly)

Same as for tail fly but without the red tag.

Black and Peacock Spider

Also one of the patterns recommended for reservoirs by Col. Drury.

HOOK. No. 7–11.

BODY. Bronze peacock herl.

HACKLE. A relatively large and soft black hen's hackle.

Shrimp

One of the most difficult creatures to imitate, and the following dressing is by Col. Joscelyn Lane, given in his book *Lake and Loch Fishing for Trout.*

HOOK. No. 12 or 13.

TYING SILK. Medium olive.

TAIL. A bunch of speckled brown partridge hackle fibres $\frac{3}{16}$-inch long, tied on the bend of the hook with fibres pointing downwards.

BODY. Of hare's ear dubbing tied well round bend of hook, padded to suggest the humped back, and as fat as possible without obstructing the gape of the hook.

HACKLE. One or more brown partridge hackles wound over the body, spaced as for ribbing, with fibres upright. Trim off closely all fibres at the sides and top, and then trim the ends of the fibres below the body level with the point of the hook. Touch the coils of quill on top of the body with varnish.

Note. For deep fishing, coils of fine wire can be wound over the hook shank before the fly is dressed.

Shrimp.

Black Lure (Black Leech)

The Tandem Hook Lure, originally evolved for estuary fishing for sea trout (fry imitation), has become very popular on the reservoirs now, particularly early in the season. Fished deep and fast it has accounted for many "bags" on Chew and elsewhere.

HOOK. Two hooks in tandem—as illustrated facing p. 33.

BODY. Black floss silk.

RIBBING. Oval or fine flat silver tinsel.

WINGS. Two black cock or hen's hackles tied back to back to form a single wing, or the other way round if a "V" effect is required.

HACKLE. Black cock or hen.

A "tag" of red wool on the rear hook is sometimes added.

Hawthorn (Sometimes spelt Hawthorne)

Another of the patterns given by Col. Joscelyn Lane, although there are several others to choose from.   His dressing is as follows:

HOOK. No. 10.

TYING SILK. Black.

BODY. Black floss tapering finely towards the tail.   This can be varnished.

RIBBING. Fine silver wire widely spaced.

HACKLE. Three or four turns of glossy black cock's hackle, tied in behind the thorax and sloping backwards.   Fibres to be as long as the hook.

THORAX. Conspicuous. Tied in last of all, using two strands of black ostrich herl.

A dry pattern of this fly is the one designed by Roger Woolley, the dressing as follows:

HOOK. No. 13.

BODY. Two black strands from a turkey tail feather tied in so that the bright black quill of them shows up most.   The ends of the two strands are tied back after forming the body, to represent the two long trailing legs of the fly.

HACKLE. Black cock.

WINGS. Palest part of a jay's wing feather.

March Brown

One of the most universally used flies, some dressings of which date back to the 17th century.   More popular on the rocky streams of northern England and of

Wales, it is sometimes called the "Cob Fly", "Brown Drake", or "Dun Drake". Dressings are numerous, and variations are many, but I think the following range will cover most anglers' needs.

Winged Wet Fly (Northern dressing)

HOOK. 13–11.

TAIL. Fibres from a brown speckled partridge hackle or tail feather.

BODY. Sandy fur from a hare's neck, or brown seal's fur.

RIB. Yellow silk or gold wire.

HACKLE. Brown partridge.

WINGS. Strips from a hen pheasant's wing feather.

Winged Dry Fly—Male

TAIL. Fibres from a brown grizzled (Cree) cock's hackle.

BODY. Hare's ear fur, mixed with a very small amount of yellow seal's fur.

RIB. Yellow tying silk.

WINGS. Darkish mottled hen pheasant or cock pheasant wing quill, tied upright.

HACKLE. Brown grizzled (Cree) cock's hackle—stiff and bright.

Winged Dry Fly—Female

Tied as for the male, but with wings of a lighter shade.

Hackled Dry Fly

TAIL. Stiff fibres from a brown grizzled (Cree) cock's hackle.

BODY. As for winged dry flies.

HACKLES. Same as for winged dry flies, but with the addition of a bright red game cock hackle (short in fibre) tied behind the cree hackle. Alternatively —A brown speckled partridge hackle wound mixed with a darkish bright blue dun cock's hackle.

MARCH BROWN VARIATIONS

Silver March Brown

TAIL. Two fibres from a brown speckled partridge hackle or speckled partridge tail feather.

BODY. Flat silver tinsel.

RIBBING.   Oval silver.
HACKLE.   Brown partridge back feather.
WINGS.   From the hen pheasant's mottled secondary wing feather.

Gold March Brown
Same as above but with gold body and ribbing.
Both these patterns are excellent for lake and sea trout fishing.

Claret March Brown
A good lake fly only differing from standard dressings in that it has a claret hackle.

Winged Wet Fly—Male
TAIL.   Two strands of brown speckled partridge feather.
BODY.   Dark hare's fur from ear.
RIB.   Yellow tying silk or gold wire.
HACKLE.   Brown speckled partridge, or brown grizzled (Cree) hen's hackle.
WINGS.   Mottled secondary feather from hen pheasant's wing.

Winged Wet Fly—Female
TAIL AND HACKLE.   As male.
BODY.   Ginger hare's fur from neck.
RIB.   Gold wire.
WINGS.   Same as for male but lighter in colour.

Hackled Wet Fly
TYING SILK.   Hot orange.
BODY.   From a hare's poll, dyed hot orange.
HACKLE.   A snipe's rump feather.

March Brown Spider
TAIL.   Two strands from a speckled partridge tail.
BODY.   Dark hare's ear, mixed with a little claret wool or seal's fur.
RIB.   Yellow or primrose tying silk.
HACKLE.   Brown speckled partridge, fairly long in fibre.

March Brown Spider (Welsh pattern)
> BODY. As above.
> RIB. Silver.
> HACKLE. As above.

I understand the name of this pattern to be Petrisen Corff Blewyn Ysgyfarnog.

March Brown Nymph
> TAIL. Two short strands of a cock pheasant's tail, or fibres of brown mallard
> shoulder feather.
> BODY. Herls from a cock pheasant's tail.
> RIB. Gold wire.
> THORAX. Hare's ear fur at shoulder.
> WING CASES. From a woodcock wing feather.   (Sometimes omitted.)
> LEGS. One turn of a small brown speckled partridge hackle.

Purple March Brown

A pattern of recent innovation, very popular in Scotland and practically always fished wet. The only deviation from the standard pattern is its purple wool or seal's fur body, ribbed with yellow silk or gold wire.

Alder

As this is the only representative of its class, there can be no derivatives. Although a water-side insect it is not bred in the water, but on rocks and rushes nearby. It is also one of the fisherman's most popular patterns, particularly as it appears in May and June when one can reasonably expect the best fishing to start. It is sometimes fished dry, but takes most of its fish as a wet fly.

> HOOK. 13–11.
> BODY. Thin peacock herl dyed magenta, or claret wool or silk ribbed with
> undyed bronze peacock herl.
> HACKLE. Black hen wound in front of wings.   Cock hackle for a dry fly.
> WINGS. Speckled brown hen wing quill, tied low over body to give the
> characteristic humped shape of the wings.
> TYING SILK. Crimson.

Gold Ribbed Hare's Ear

Another "champion" fly with a fine reputation all over the U.K., fished wet or dry. It is thought to represent the nymph in the process of shedding its shuck, and should therefore be fished only slightly submerged for the best results.

HOOK. No. 14–16.
BODY. Dark fur from the root of the hare's ear spun on yellow silk.
RIBBING. Fine flat gold tinsel.
HACKLE. Long strands of the body material picked out with the dubbing needle.
WHISKS. Three strands as hackle.

If a winged pattern is preferred, these should be formed of fibres from a starling's primary wing feather, low over the body for the wet fly, upright and double for the dry fly.

Snipe and Purple

A standard pattern for Yorkshire and the north generally, and a particularly good lake pattern elsewhere.

HOOK. No. 14–15.
BODY. Purple floss.
HACKLE. Small feather from the outside of a Snipe's wing, taken from as near the joint as possible.

Another version is the "Snipe and Yellow", not quite as popular but often more effective on very cold days. The hackle is a dun feather from the back of a snipe's wing, and the body is formed of either yellow or straw coloured silk.

Greenwell (Greenwell's Glory)

Invented by Canon William Greenwell of Durham, this is probably the best known of this whole list. In fact it is more likely the most well-known fly of all! It is effective no matter which of the duns the fish may be taking, and is a pattern which can be fished with confidence during the entire season. The dressing can be varied to suit particular conditions, but the original was as follows:

HOOK. No. 14.
BODY. Yellow silk (sometimes ribbed with fine gold wire).
HACKLE. Light Coch-y-bondhu, cock or hen.
WINGS. Hen blackbird wing feather.

The yellow silk of the body is more often than not waxed with cobblers wax to impart an olive hue, and what is called a "Furnace" hackle is usually used in place of the Coch-y-bondhu. The furnace hackle does not have the black tips of the Coch-y-bondhu.

For a dry hackled pattern, a blue dun cock's hackle should be wound with a furnace cock, and tail consisting of a few fibres of furnace cock hackle also added.

This fly is also a successful lake pattern, and larger versions (up to size 8 old scale) are very popular in New Zealand. The New Zealand anglers add either a bright red tag or a tail of golden pheasant tippet fibres.

Partridge and Yellow

Another standard North Country pattern for both trout and grayling, and also effective as a lake fly. Sometimes called "Partridge Spider".

HOOK. No. 14.
BODY. Yellow floss silk.
RIBBING (optional). Flat gold tinsel.
HACKLE. Partridge breast feather.

The "Partridge and Orange" is another version, having an orange silk body instead of yellow, and a darker hackle, from the back of the partridge.

Cardinal

BODY. Red floss silk, ribbed fine gold wire.
WINGS. Dyed red swan, ibis or duck.
HACKLE. Dyed same colour as wings.
TAIL. Red ibis.

Professor

BODY. Yellow tying or floss silk, ribbed either gold tinsel or black tying silk.
WINGS. From the breast feather of a grey mallard.
HACKLE. Natural ginger cock's.
TAIL. A few long fibres of red ibis feather.

Jungle Cock

BODY. Black floss silk, ribbed gold wire.
WINGS. Two jungle cock neck feathers.
HACKLE. Black cock's.
TAIL. Three or four fibres of a golden pheasant tippet feather.

Blue Kingfisher

BODY. Flat silver tinsel, ribbed fine silver oval.
WINGS. Two breast feathers of the kingfisher, left untrimmed.
HACKLE. Dyed light blue cock's.

Silver Saltoun

BODY. Black tying silk, ribbed fine silver wire.
WINGS. Lightest starling wing-feather.
HACKLE. Black.
TAIL. Three whisks as hackle.

Bustard and Red

BODY.   Bright red seals fur, ribbed fine
gold wire.

WINGS.   From the bustard wing feather.

HACKLE.   Natural blood-red hen,
sparsely dressed.

TAIL.   A small golden pheasant crest
feather.

Col. Downman's Fancy

BODY.   Black floss silk, ribbed silver
tinsel.

WINGS.   Jay wing, with small jungle
cock each side.

HACKLE.   Black.

TAIL.   Teal fibres.

Little's Fancy

BODY.   Flat silver tinsel.

WINGS.   Hen pheasant centre tail.

HACKLE.   Ginger.

TAIL.   Golden pheasant crest feather.

Blue Zulu

BODY.   Black dubbing ribbed fine silver
tinsel.

HACKLE.   Dyed blue.

TAIL.   Red wool.

Watson's Fancy

BODY.   Half red and half black floss or
dubbing ribbed silver tinsel.

WINGS.   From crow wing, with small
jungle cock feather each side.

HACKLE.   Black.

TAIL.   Small golden pheasant crest
feather.

Fiery Brown

BODY.   Fiery brown seals fur, ribbed
gold oval.

WINGS.   Brown mallard.

HACKLE.   Fiery brown.

TAIL.   Tippet fibres.

TAG.   Orange floss.

Iron Blue Nymph

HOOK.   16.

WHISKS.   Three short fibres from a white cock's hackle.

BODY.   Mole fur spun on claret tying silk.

THORAX.   Mole fur.

WING CASES.   Waterhen's secondary wing feather.

LEGS.   One turn of a short fibred dark blue dun hen's hackle.

Mayfly Nymphs

These should be tied fairly heavily as the mayfly numph is a good sized insect.
There are many patterns but the following three should meet most requirements.

No. 1.

    HOOK.   11–9, long-shanked.

    TAIL.   Three short strands from a cock pheasant's tail feather.

    BODY AND THORAX.   Brown olive seal's fur.

    RIB.   Oval gold tinsel.

    WING CASE.   From a hen pheasant's tail feather.   Dark as possible.

    LEGS.   Brown partridge back feather.

No. 2.

    TAIL.   As for No. 1.

    BODY.   Three turns at tail end of dirty yellow seal's fur.   The remainder and thorax of brown olive seal's fur.

    RIB.   Yellow silk, thicker than the normal tying silk.

    WING CASE.   As for No. 1.

    LEGS.   A mottled feather from a hen pheasant's neck.

No. 3.

    TAIL.   As for Nos. 1 and 2.

    BODY AND THORAX.   Pale buff seal's fur.

    RIB.   Oval gold tinsel.

    WING CASE.   As for Nos. 1 and 2.

    LEGS.   Dark brown grouse hackle.

Wet Mayflies

More often than not these are used at the commencement of the rise while the fly is hatching, and should therefore be fished semi-submerged.

No. 1.

    HOOK.   11–9, long-shanked.

    TAILS.   Three strands from a cock pheasant's tail.

    BODY.   Dyed yellow lamb's wool.

    RIB.   Oval gold tinsel.

    LEGS.   Hen pheasant neck feather dyed yellow, or undyed.

    WINGS.   Speckled grey mallard feather dyed yellow.

No. 2.

    TAILS.   As for No. 1.

    BODY.   As for No. 1.

    RIB.   As for No. 1.

    LEGS.   Ginger cock's hackle, dyed yellow.

    WINGS.   Speckled grey mallard feather dyed greenish-yellow.

No. 3.
  TAILS.   As for Nos. 1 and 2.
  BODY.   Buff yellow floss silk.
  RIB.   Oval gold tinsel.
  LEGS.   Brown grouse hackle.
  WINGS.   Grizzle cock hackle dyed greenish-yellow.

Amber Nymph

Another of Dr. Bell's patterns for lake fishing, of which there are two versions. They have been very successful in both Blagdon and Chew Valley lakes.

"Large Amber Nymph" for use in May and June and usually the first dropper, and the "Small Amber Nymph" for use in July.

  HOOK.   No. 11 10.   For the large pattern.   No. 12 for the small.
  BODY.   Amber yellow floss silk or seal's fur tied rather thick.
  THORAX.   Brown floss silk or seal's fur, approximately one-third the length of the body.
  WING CASE.   A strip of any grey-brown feather, tied in at the tail and finished behind the thorax.
  LEGS.   A few fibres of pale honey hens hackle, tied in under the head and extending backwards.

The only difference in the smaller pattern is that the thorax should be of hot orange floss silk or seal's fur.

Buzzer Nymph

From the same stable as the Amber Nymph, this should be fished in June and from mid-August to the end of September.

  HOOK.   No. 12 10.
  BODY.   Black floss silk taken partly round the bend of the hook.
  RIBBING.   Flat gold tinsel.
  WINGS.   A short tuft of white floss silk tied in just behind the head, about $\frac{1}{8}$-inch long.
  LEGS.   A few fibres of brown mallard shoulder feather tied in under the head and sloping backwards.

Lake Olive Nymph

This is another of Col. Joscelyn Lane's patterns, and a "must" for all lake fishermen.

HOOK. No. 12.

TYING SILK. Golden olive.

TAIL. A bunch of dyed olive cock hackle fibres, about $\frac{1}{4}$-inch long.

ABDOMEN. Olive silk or 3X nylon, very thin at tail end and thickening gradually up to thorax.

THORAX. Darker and thicker than the body, but not ball-shaped.

RIBBING. Fine gold wire.

HACKLE. A small bunch of dyed olive cock hackle fibres, tied in under the throat, and with most of the fibres lying back close along the body.

Col. Lane recommends a darker variation of the dressing for spring fishing, and for an imitation of the nymph on the point of hatching he plumps for our old friend the "Gold Ribbed Hare's Ear" discussed earlier.

DEMOISELLE DRAGON-FLY NYMPH

Regarded by Col. Lane as one of the most useful all-round patterns for lake fishing, together with the "Large Dragon-Fly Nymph", the dressing of which I also give here.

Demoiselle

HOOK. No. 10.

TYING SILK. Golden olive.

TAIL. A big bunch of dyed olive cock's hackle fibres, cut off square to a length of $\frac{1}{4}$ inch.

BODY AND THORAX. Carrot shaped. Of olive floss silk or 3X Nylon, tapering from tail up to a full $\frac{1}{8}$ inch at thorax.

RIBBING. Finest gold wire ending short of thorax.

LEG. A bunch of dyed olive cock hackles fibres, tied in under the throat to lie close beneath body.

Large Nymph

HOOK. No. 10 9.

TYING SILK. Green.

TAIL. Three lengths of thick knitting wool $\frac{1}{4}$-inch long. One medium green and two nigger brown.

BODY. Two pieces of the same wool, one medium green and the other nigger brown, twisted together and wound on tightly. The body should be $\frac{1}{4}$-inch thick in the middle and taper at both ends, and be tied down with open turns of the tying silk.

HACKLE. One turn of a brown partridge back feather dyed very dark green.

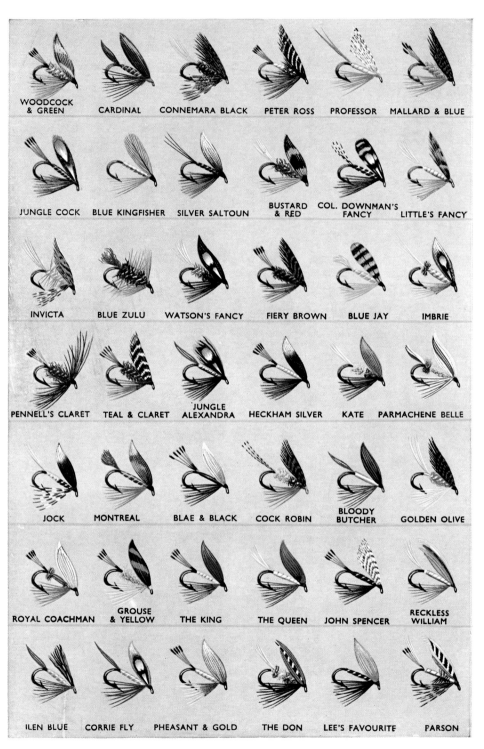

STANDARD LAKE FLIES
TIED BY JOHN VENIARD

Blue Jay

BODY. Light blue floss, ribbed fine gold wire.

WINGS. The blue feather from a jay wing.

HACKLE. Light blue same colour as body.

TAIL. Leave a short length of the floss used for the body and tease it out with a dubbing needle.

Imbrie

BODY. White floss silk, ribbed flat gold tinsel, with two tags at the tail end—the first of green peacock herl and the second of flat gold tinsel.

WINGS. Dark starling wing feather with an inset of jungle cock feather on each side.

HACKLE. Natural light red or ginger cock's.

TAIL. Three long fibres from the crest feather of a golden pheasant.

Broughton's Point

BODY. Claret tying silk.

WINGS. From the wing feather of a starling.

HACKLE. Mixed black and dyed scarlet cock's.

Cairn's Fancy

BODY. Blue floss silk, ribbed fine flat silver tinsel.

WINGS. Starling.

HACKLE. Black hen.

Pennell's Claret

BODY. Claret seals fur ribbed fine gold wire or oval tinsel.

HACKLE. A long fibred furnace cock's.

TAIL. Tippet fibres and crest fibres.

Teal and Claret

BODY. Claret dubbing ribbed gold tinsel.

WINGS. Teal breast.

HACKLE. Claret.

TAIL. Tippet fibres.

Heckham Silver

BODY. Flat silver tinsel, ribbed fine silver oval.

WINGS. The white tipped feather from a wild duck wing.

HACKLE. Black.

TAIL. Three or four fibres of the golden pheasant tippet feather.

Kate

BODY. Halved, the tail end being canary yellow and the remainder scarlet seals fur. The whole body is ribbed with oval gold tinsel.

WINGS. From the fawny brown feathers on the jay's wing.

HACKLE. Natural black cock's.

TAIL. Whole feather of a golden pheasant crest.

Parmachene Belle

BODY. Yellow floss silk or wool, ribbed flat gold tinsel.

WINGS. White duck or swan with a stripe of red ibis feather on each side, the ibis should be about half the width of the duck or swan.

HACKLE. Dyed scarlet cock's mixed with white cock's.

TAIL. Red and white duck.

Jock

BODY. Halved, the tail end being of yellow and the remainder black floss silk, the whole body is ribbed with fine gold oval tinsel.

WINGS. The white tipped feather from a wild duck wing.

HACKLE. The small spotted guinea fowl hackle (Gallena).

TAIL. Smallest whole feather of a golden pheasant crest.

Montreal

BODY. Red floss silk, ribbed gold wire.

WINGS. From the wing feather of a woodcock.

HACKLE. Light red.

TAIL. A piece of the floss silk used for the body.

Blae and Black

BODY. Black floss, wool or seals fur.

WINGS. Wild duck wing-feather.

HACKLE. Black hen.

TAIL. A few fibres of golden pheasant tippet.

Cock Robin

BODY. First half golden olive, second half scarlet, ribbed oval gold tinsel.

WING. Brown mallard.

HACKLE. Natural dark red cock.

TAIL. Three strands of brown mallard.

The King

BODY. Gold tinsel.

WINGS. Swan on duck dyed crimson.

HACKLE. Royal blue.

TAIL. Golden pheasant tippet.

The Queen

BODY. Silver tinsel.

WINGS. Swan or duck dyed royal blue.

HACKLE. Crimson.

TAIL. Golden pheasant crest.

John Spencer

BODY. Black floss, ribbed silver oval tinsel.

WINGS. Grey mallard breast feather.

HACKLE. Black.

TAIL. Golden pheasant tippet.

Reckless William

BODY. Half flat silver tinsel, half pink floss silk.

WINGS. Emerald green swan, hen pheasant centre tail dyed emerald green outside, topping over all.

HACKLE. Orange cock.

TAIL. Golden pheasant crest feather.

Ilen Blue

BODY. Gold tinsel ribbed gold oval.

WINGS. Fibres of blue peacock feather.

HACKLE. Red.

TAIL. Ibis.

Corrie Fly

BODY. Silver tinsel, ribbed silver wire.

WINGS. Grey mallard, wing quill, with jungle cock each side.

HACKLE. Bright claret.

TAIL. Scarlet ibis.

Pheasant and Gold

BODY. Flat gold tinsel, ribbed fine gold oval.

WINGS. From the quill feather of the hen pheasant wing.

HACKLE. Soft feather from front of hen pheasant wing.

TAIL. Whisks of golden pheasant tippet.

The Don

BODY. One-third at tail yellow, two-thirds claret seals fur ribbed gold oval.

WINGS. Lightly dressed, dun turkey with a strip of teal each side.

HACKLE. Black.

TAG. Silver twist and yellow floss.

TAIL. Topping.

BUTT. Green peacock herl.

Lee's Favourite

BODY. Black floss, ribbed flat silver.

WINGS. Jay wing.

HACKLE. Black.

Parson

BODY. Flat silver tinsel, ribbed fine silver oval.

WINGS. Heavily marked teal, over a foundation of dyed yellow and scarlet swan feather. A golden pheasant crest over the back of the wing.

HACKLE. Black cock's with a throat hackle of blue jay wing feather.

TAIL. Mixed golden pheasant crest and tippet feather.

Professor

BODY. Yellow tying or floss silk, ribbed either gold tinsel or black tying silk.

WINGS. From the breast feather of a grey mallard.

HACKLE. Natural ginger cock's.

TAIL. A few long fibres of red ibis feather.

Zulu

BODY. Black wool or seals fur, ribbed fine flat silver tinsel.

HACKLE. Black cock's.

TAIL. Red ibis feather or red wool.

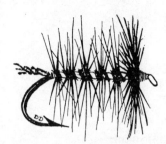

Black Zulu.

Black Duck Fly (dry)
(Alternate names: "Black Midge" or "Black Buzzer".)
HOOK. No. 13 or 14.
BODY. Black floss, thicker at shoulder.
WINGS. Two dun or cream cock hackle points tied sloping backwards.
HACKLE. Rusty black cock, short in fibre, tied in front of wings.

Black Duck Fly (wet)
(See also "Buzzer Nymph".)
HOOK. No. 12–14.
BODY. Black silk or wool, wound thicker at shoulder.
HACKLE. Black cock.
WING. Starling wing quill fibres, tied short, divided, and inclined towards tail.

Large Olive Midge (dry)
("Olive Buzzer")
HOOK. No. 12–14.
BODY. Hare's ear mixed with olive seal's fur.
BODY HACKLE. Cream cock, or cream badger cock (light centre).
SHOULDER HACKLE. Cream badger cock tied spent.

Olive Buzzer
(See "Large Olive Midge".)

Black Buzzer
(See "Black Duck Fly".)

Gold Zulu
TAIL. Red wool.
BODY. Bronze peacock herl.
RIB. Fine flat gold tinsel.
HACKLE. Coch-y-bondhu from shoulder to tail.

Black Midge
(See "Black Duck Fly".)

Olive Midge
(See "Olive Duck Fly".)

Olive Duck Fly (dry)
HOOK. No. 12–13.
BODY. Olive floss silk or swan herl dyed pale green olive.
WINGS. Two blue dun or cream cock hackle points tied sloping backwards over hook.
RIB. Gold wire.
HACKLE. Pale grizzle or rusty dun cock, tied in front of wing.

Bridgett's Black
(Wet lake fly—for chironomid representation.)
TAIL. Two fibres from a guinea-fowl hackle.
BODY. Black ostrich herl.
RIB. Fine silver wire.
HACKLE. Guinea fowl.

Burleigh (Loch Leven fly)
TAIL. Ginger hackle fibres (or tippet).

BODY. Yellow tying silk well waxed to make it olive.
RIB. Silver wire.
HACKLE. Ginger.
WINGS. Starling wing feather, tied low over body in sedge style.

John Storey

TAIL. Fibres from a red cock's hackle.
BODY. Thin peacock herl.
RIB. Scarlet tying silk.
HACKLE. Red.
WING. Grey Mallard flank.

Grouse and Purple

TAIL. Golden pheasant tippet fibres.
BODY. Purple seal fur.
RIB. Oval gold tinsel.
HACKLE. Black.
WING. Grouse tail feather.

Cinnamon and Gold

TAIL. Tippet fibres (or fibres of cinnamon coloured hackle).
BODY. Flat gold.
RIB. Gold wire.
HACKLE. Cinnamon brown.
WING. Cinnamon hen wing quill.

Aylott's Orange

BODY. Orange D.F.M. wool or seal fur.
HACKLE. Brown hen (natural).
HEAD. Bronze peacock herl.

Don's Perch Fry

(Designed by Don Downs, producer of the black and white drawings in this book.)
Illustrated in frontispiece.
TAIL. Cream hackle fibres.
BODY. White silk covered by PVC (Polystickle style).
HACKLE. "Beard "of scarlet hen hackle fibres.
WING. Two light red hen's hackles back to back—first "barred" with a black felt-tipped pen.

Wave Moth

This is the Col. J. T. H. Lane pattern.
HOOK. No. 12. No. 10 to imitate a Mayfly, or for night fishing.
TYING SILK. Straw.
BODY. Honey cock hackle, wound close with coils touching but not overlapping. Trim all fibres close to quill.
HACKLE. Wound over body—starting approx. half way along shank, close turns to give a "full" hackle. A yellowish badger cock hackle, with fibres as long as the hook.

Pheasant Tail Nymph

TAIL. Fibres of Honey cock hackle—short.
BODY. Fibres from a cock pheasant tail. Good red colour.
RIB. Gold or copper wire.
HACKLE. Honey. (Body to be thicker at thorax).

DAPPING FLIES

A FORM of "dapping" practised mainly on the wind-swept lakes of Scotland and Ireland is a most interesting and rewarding method of angling.

A long (14 ft.) rod is the customary weapon used, the reel loaded with plenty of backing, to which is attached a length of light but stout floss silk. The floss line should be quite long, so that the backing does not have to be let out during the actual "dapping".

The fly is attached to the "blow line", as the floss is called, by a short length of gut or nylon, fairly stout, as this method of fishing seems to bring the big ones to the surface.

The line is not laid on the water as in normal casting, but should belly out in the wind, allowing the fly to "dap" on the surface like a natural insect.

Mayfly imitations can be used at the appropriate time when fishing the Irish loughs, but the usual patterns for this type of fishing are large heavily hackled ones.

Sometimes they are of the "palmer" type or hackled in the front only, but whichever type is used, *several* hackles must be wound together to ensure full and heavy hackling.

One or two patterns are given here for guidance, but a range of different-coloured types can be made merely by altering the hackle colour. Usual mayfly hackled patterns can be used, adapting them by increasing the amount of hackle used. Three patterns are illustrated in the coloured plate facing page 80.

Scots Grey

TAIL. Fibres from a stiff grizzle hackle.
BODY. Blue dun seal's fur.
RIB. Fine flat silver tinsel (for lightness).
HACKLE. Three grizzle cock hackles, at front only.

Red Palmer

TAIL. None.
BODY. Dyed red seal's fur.
RIB. Fine gold wire.
HACKLE. Several natural red game hackles wound "palmer" from bend to eye of hook.

Black Pennell

(other colours—brown, yellow, green).
TAG. Fine flat silver tinsel.
TAIL. Tippet fibres.
BODY. Black floss silk, very thin.
RIB. Fine flat silver tinsel.
HACKLE. Two or three black cock hackles at front only (natural red game or furnace as alternatives).
HOOK. No. 8-10, 12.

Grey Wulf

A dapping version of the famous American dry fly.
TAIL. Brown bucktail fibres.
BODY. Blue grey wool.
WINGS. A bunch of grey squirrel tail fibres, tied forward and split.
HACKLE. Two or three stiff blue dun hackles, wound at front only.

The wings can be tied on first on this pattern, and their roots incorporated into the body.

Daddy Longlegs

BODY. Brown floss, raffia, or raffine.
LEGS. Knotted pheasant tail fibres, tied in a bunch, sloping backwards, and then divided.
WINGS AND HACKLE. Two gingery hackles wound together, the two points tied in "spent" to form the wings.
TYING SILK. Brown.
HOOK. No. 8-10 up-eye.

THE JOHN HENDERSON PATTERNS

THE ensuing pages, contributed by John Henderson, appeared originally in a series of articles contributed by the author to the *Journal* of the Fly Fishers' Club. On the suggestion of some members of the club they were collected in the form of a booklet. A limited number were printed privately and distributed by the author to members of the Club who were keen on fly-tying, and also to his friends who were keen fly-fishers and fly-dressers. Mr. Henderson, together with the editor (D. J. Berry) of the Fly Fishers' Club *Journal* very kindly gave me permission to reproduce the contents of the booklet, and I was also very happy to include some patterns in the coloured illustrations, tied by Mr. Henderson himself.

All his patterns are representations of natural insects, following more in the footsteps of Halford, Skues, C. F. Walker and others of equal fame who have applied entymological knowledge to their fly dressing, rather than some of the more modern school who lean towards the attractor type of fly rather than the imitation of the natural.

If one considers all the personal notes he has added to this list of dressings, i.e. when where and how to fish, the fund of knowledge contained within this section of the book will be of value to lake fishermen for generations to come, and I personally am very pleased to be in a position to bring his work to the notice of more lake fishermen than he himself may have considered possible.

JOHN VENIARD.

"FLY FISHING ON LAKES AND RESERVOIRS
WITH PARTICULAR REFERENCE TO DRY-FLY AND NYMPH FISHING"

by John Henderson

As the ever increasing demand for more water goes on in this country, so it becomes necessary to have more reservoirs and hardly a year passes without hearing of a new one being constructed. As the number of them increase so does the number of fly-fishers increase, and at the same time, owing to pollution, water extraction, and other causes, the available fishing on rivers is on the decrease.

If conditions continue to deteriorate on rivers, where the best of the fly-fishing is now in private hands, it will not be long before the only fly-fishing available to the angling public will be on reservoirs. Although some reservoirs contain only coarse fish, most of them are stocked with trout and fly-fishing is available on most of them.

The types of reservoirs vary considerably depending on the nature of the country and the geological formation in which they are situated. I am therefore dividing them into two types namely:

1. Upland — those in the hilly country of Wales and the north.
2. Lowlands — those in the soft undulating country of the south.

Typical examples of upland reservoirs are Lake Vyrnwy in North Wales which supplies Liverpool with water and the chain of reservoirs in the Elan and Claerwen Valleys of mid-Wales which supply Birmingham with water. These are all in steep valleys of the Silurian rocks. Others in the Brecknock Beacons of South Wales are in valleys not too steep and rugged, being situated in the Old Red Sandstones.

Typical examples of lowland reservoirs are Blagdon, Chew, Sutton Bingham, and Weir Wood. There are many others in the South midlands—particularly in the Charnwood Forest area. All these contain much more under-water food than the Upland reservoirs, probably because some of them are in or near limestone, and their waters being more alkaline can support a much greater quantity of animals and the trout grow to a larger size than those in upland reservoirs.

Owing to there being more available food below the surface, trout in these lowland reservoirs become rather fixed in their habits and feed on the various creatures forming their under water food such as nymphs of various kinds, corixa, mites, snails, caddis grubs, shrimps, minnows, sticklebacks, etc. It, therefore requires an abnormal amount of floating insects, whether they are flies or beetles, to bring them up to feed at the surface.

Unless trout are seen to be rising to something on the surface, it is not much use fishing with the dry-fly as it is restricted to fishing on the surface only. The wet-fly on the other hand has much greater scope for catching fish as the fly or flies can be fished near the surface, in mid water or as near the bottom as possible. The wet-fly fisherman will therefore maintain, and with some reason, that the wet-fly is the most efficient allround method for catching fish on lakes and reservoirs. In considering the above pros and cons, the pros are definitely in favour of wet-fly. The wet-fly man prefers and can fish under any conditions whether fish are seen to be rising or not. The dry-fly man prefers to fish dry-fly whenever possible, but when fish are not seen to be rising or there is too strong a wind, only then, when these adverse conditions occur, is he obliged to have recourse to the wet-fly. Although his fishing is therefore to some extent restricted, the dry-fly man is likely to have more interesting fishing when conditions are favourable for his method, that is, some fish rising and not too strong a breeze.

Some anglers prefer fishing from a boat while others prefer bank fishing. As feeding fish are usually cruising about close to the shore, bank angling is preferred by many, for the angler is then completely independent and free to do as he likes, as he is not under the control of the boatman as so often happens when fishing from a boat.

Assuming an angler with a preference to dry-fly fishing arrives at a reservoir to fish, it will probably be at the dam end. He should carefully observe the conditions from the dam and decide which should be the best shore to fish from. This will depend largely upon the force and direction of the wind. If the wind is blowing over the dam and up the reservoir, there is usually a calm area above the dam and with an eddying undercurrent immediately above the dam, a number of flies and insects born by the wind over the dam from the valley below, will drop in the calm area, so it is here particularly at the two angles made by the dam and the shores at each end, that trout are cruising round on the look out for surface food. If the breeze blowing over the dam is only slight there is likely to be a fairly large extent of calm water above it. Further observation may show that the calm water stretches further along one shore than the other. This indicates that the shore having the longest stretch of calm water is more sheltered than the other. It follows that the less sheltered shore, having the breeze blowing across to it from the dam, is likely to have air born insects which will tend to drift on to this shore. Therefore the chances for catching a fish here should be better than on the more sheltered shore. When trout are rising in the calm water above the dam, they generally cruise along on a certain beat, and as they swim along they suck down any flies they see. The tactics of the angler is to place his fly well ahead of the trout and in line with its beat. The trout continues its course towards his fly, sucking down flies as it comes nearer until his should be the next—after what appears to be ages, but actually may be a matter of a few seconds, his fly disappears and the angler is into his fish.

If no fish are showing in the calm stretch above the dam, the angler should walk along the shore to where the calm water gives way to a ripple. Should a fish be seen to rise here within casting distance from the shore, he casts his fly well ahead of the rise, making allowance for the wind blowing the cast towards the fish which is travelling against the wind towards his fly, which in all probability, will be taken by the trout as it meets it. This procedure of drifting the fly the angler keeping pace with it on the shore can be continued and should a fish be seen to rise ahead of him, he can cast his fly to intercept the fish. Sometimes fish will rise quite close to the shore.

Should the wind be blowing down the reservoir towards the dam, the wet-fly angler can start into fish any length of the shore, paying particular attention to points of land which jut out into the reservoir where fish are often on the look out for food. If a dry-fly angler, he can go either to the top or to some point of land on either shore which gives some shelter to a stretch of water and proceed to fish by drifting his fly with the wind as already described. When a steady breeze is blowing, lines of foam often form and wind born flies seem to collect in them and trout are often found there on the look out, the angler therefore should endeavour to drift his fly along one of them.

In some reservoirs there will be hedges or stone walls which were the boundaries of fields before the valley was flooded and which now disappear under the surface at intervals along the shores. These are sure lurking places for a trout, so when fishing past them, they should be given particular attention.

WEATHER CONDITIONS

The ideal weather conditions for fly-fishing on reservoirs and lakes are a soft steady breeze, a cloudy sky with an occasional burst of sunshine. These should not be very unusual conditions but it is surprising how seldom they occur. On a bright sunny day with complete lack of cloud, there is little chance of catching a trout with a dry-fly until the sun has sunk behind the hills. A bright sun with a strong wind drives every fish from the shallow shores into the shade of deep water, where they remain until the sun goes down. West shores should be the most productive for evening fishing as they are the first to get in the shade and trout will begin to feed along them earlier than along the eastern shores.

A bright sun with a slight ripple is not so hopeless if there is fly on the water and fish rising, but at least half the fish that rise to the dry-fly will shy off as they are about to take. The reason for this sudden fright just as they are breaking the surface to take the fly may be caused by the shadow of the gut passing over their eyes or perhaps they can feel the shadow on their bodies. In bright sunshine, therefore, the only positions in which the fish can take the fly and not come in contact with this shadow are at right angles to the cast and directly opposite and away from the cast.

THE SURFACE FOOD OF TROUT

Although the duns (*Ephemeroptera*) are the most important surface food for trout on rivers, this is not so on reservoirs where, in addition to the non-biting midges, it consists mostly of land insects falling on the surface. However, on many lakes there are good hatches of fly, for instance, on the limestone loughs of Ireland there are great hatches of Mayfly which also occur on some of the lakes of the Lake District and on some of the lochs of Scotland as far north as Sutherland where in the areas of Durness limestone, there are several lochs which have fairly big hatches. The Lake Olive and Claret Dun are to be found on many lakes in Ireland and Wales also in the Lake District and in Scotland.

On reservoirs, however, the most important surface food of trout are the non-biting Midges which in numbers far exceed any other water bred fly, the commonest being the Black Midge, among others which are fairly common is the Green Midge, the Olive Midge and Grey Midge. As these flies, their larvae and nymphs are one of the main food supplies of trout in reservoirs, I will describe them in more detail later under Fly-Dressings.

The next in importance are the Sedges or Caddis Flies which appear in great numbers during the summer evenings, which trout feed on as well as on their larvae and pupae.

The Willow Fly is the only member of the Stone Fly family that appears in any quantity, particularly on upland reservoirs.

The Alder is well known to most fishermen, whether on river or lake, it is fairly numerous on some reservoirs during May and June but varies in numbers from year to year. It does not seem to be in such numbers in this country as' in parts of the continent such as in Denmark and Sweden where they sometimes occur in enormous quantities.

Of the land flies which fall on the surface of the water the Bibionidae are perhaps the most important, even more so on lakes and reservoirs than on rivers. The first to appear is the Black Gnat (*Bibio johanis*), towards the end of April and through May. About the same time the Hawthorn Fly (*Bibio marki*) begins to show in May and lasts for about a fortnight. Another Bibio, about half way in size between the Black Gnat and the Hawthorn Fly occurs sometimes in May and June and is described by Aldam, who names it the "Small Caterpillar". If the lake or reservoir is situated in heather country, the Heather Fly (*B. pomomae*) may appear in August and September and when it does, it usually comes in enormous numbers. Andrew Lang in his *Angling Sketches* describes such an occurrence when fishing a small loch among the hills of Selkirkshire where the local name for the fly is the "Bloody Doctor".

John Beever in his *Practical Fly Fishing* also describes an enormous flight of these flies in September near Coniston in the Lake District.

BEETLES

These exceed all the other land insects which fall on the surface of the water. They range in size from the Cockchafer or May Bug of 1 inch to $1\frac{1}{2}$-inch in length, to the smallest Staph of not more than $\frac{1}{8}$-inch. "Staphs" being the name given to them by beetle collectors (*Coleopterists*) being short for Staphylinidae which extensive family contains most of the bettles with short wing cases (*Brachelytra*). Between these are a great number of beetles including the Cochybonddu beetle or Marlow Buzz, the larger Staphs, Ground beetles, Soldier and Sailor beetles, the Click beetles or Skipjacks, and if there are trees along the shore, there is likely to be some leaf weevils dropping on the water during the summer.

MOTHS

The small light coloured moth known as the grass moth is the most likely one to be blown on to the surface and when in sufficient numbers, trout often rise to them well.

LIST OF INSECTS MOST LIKELY TO OCCUR IN EACH MONTH
OF THE FISHING SEASON

APRIL.—Small beetles, small Stone fly, Chironomus tentans.

MAY.—Alders, Mayflies, Lake Olives, Claret Duns, Sedges, Cockchafers, Cochybonddus, Staphs, Soldier and Sailor beetles, Skipjacks and other small beetles including weevils, Black Gnats, Hawthorn flies, and Chironomids.

JUNE.—Alders, Mayflies, Lake Olives, Cockchafers, Cochybonddus, Skipjacks, quantities of small beetles mostly Staphs and weevils, Black Gnats and in evenings sedges and Chironomids.

JULY.—During this month there is usually not sufficient surface food during the day to bring the trout up to feed on it. Should a breeze come on, however, there may be a few land flies and other insects blown on to the surface such as Daddy-long-legs, in the evenings sedges and Chironomids.

AUGUST.—During the day, Daddy-long-legs, Heather Fly, Flying Ants. In the evening, Chironomids, black and brown Silver-horns, and other larger sedges.

SEPTEMBER.—During the day, Flying Ants, Willow Fly, Beetles, particularly medium Staphs. In the evenings, black and brown Silver-horns and other larger sedges, a few Chironomids.

NOTE.—On Weir Wood reservoir, during the summer months, although there are some Chironomus tentans, the commonest of the non-biting midges is one smaller than C. tentans and when seen on the water appear to be of a light grey colour, the body however is opaque, perhaps almost transparent. This seems to be the same fly that C. F. Walker describes in his *Lake Flies and Their Imitation* which he has named "The Phantom Midge". The trout feed on them well and from autopsies they seem to take them as they are hatching out at the surface.

FLY DRESSINGS

MAYFLIES

When one considers the infinite pains taken by fly-dressers to obtain an exact imitation of say an olive dun, particularly its colours; how is it that in the case of the Mayfly, there is such a diversity of colours and sizes in both the body and wings? Every fly-fisher seems to have his own particular fancy, some preferring a dark coloured fly, while others a light coloured one, some even going so far as to like pink bodies and orange in the hackles.

Several experienced fly-fishers I have known, preferred to fish with a dark fly, for instance G. Lloyd Dicken, one of the early members of the Flyfishers Club, had his own particular pattern which he dressed with Guinea fowl's feathers, dyed olive green, as wings, a ginger hackle and an olive body, the whole fly having a very dark appearance. Another old member of the club, Arthur Severn, had a great liking for the "Marquis", this has a black body but has a white ribbing and ginger and mallard hackle.

Arthur Gibbs in his book *A Cotswold Village* has this to say about Mayflies: "It is ten to one that those in the shops are too light both in the body and the wings; the Mayflies usually sold are likewise too big, about half life size is quite big enough for the artificial fly and as a general rule they cannot be too dark. Mottled grey for your wings and a brown hackle with a dark rather than a straw coloured body, is the kind of fly we find the most killing on the upper Coln".

Courtney Williams in his *Dictionary of Trout Flies* says he finds sometimes that trout prefer light coloured dressings with almost white bodies.

My own preference is for a darkish fly but I am inclined to think that light conditions and reflected light are the deciding factors which cause trout to take the artificials of different colours according to the light conditions. It is therefore up to the angler to put on the fly which he has found from experience to be suitable for the particular light conditions.

I fished the Coln at Whelford a few miles below Fairford since my boyhood days and was never very successful with the Mayfly, my recollections being that I caught as many trout on the Welshman's Button and the Black Gnat as I did on the Mayfly. However, during the last few seasons I fished the Coln, I tied some flies similar to a fly I tied for Lough Arrow in 1906-7 and which the trout took well there. This fly proved to be equally successful on the Coln, and so I now give its dressing in detail as well as the dressing of my father's pattern of the Spent Drake, this I have modified to some extent by giving it a body hackle for floatation purposes and do not use the small piece of rubber tubing to keep the wing hackles clear while dressing the body.

Mayfly, Green Drake with Split Hackle Fan Wings

HOOK.   Long-shanked Mayfly, Nos. 5 or 6 (Veniard's Nos. 9 or 10).

SILK.   Pale yellow.

WHISKS.   Three fibres from a cock pheasant's tail feather.

BODY.   Seal's fur mixture (Pale buff mixed with a very little Fiery Brown and Pale Olive).

BODY HACKLE.   Light Plymouth Rock cock dyed pale olive.

RIBBING.   Gold tinsel with brown Nylusta or tying silk twisted round it.

HACKLE (WINGS).   Large light dun cock's, dyed light olive or a mixture of half lemon and half slate.

HACKLES (LEGS).   Light Plymouth Rock cock's dyed light olive.

METHOD OF DRESSING

After tying in the whisks and ribbing at bend of hook and dubbing the body, the body hackle is tied in by stem at shoulder and twisted down body spirally to tail where it is fixed by ribbing which is then twisted up body to shoulder and fixed by two half hitches.   The body now being finished, the large hackle for the wings is tied in by the stem at the shoulder and taken not more than six turns round the shank then fixed with two half hitches, the hackle fibres are now brought up in a bunch above the shank, hold them all together with finger and thumb, pass the tying silk round the back of them, then round under the shank and up to the front where a turn of the silk is made followed by two half hitches. The turn or bight of silk behind the fibres should be just sufficiently tight to keep the bunched together fibres upright.   Now divide them in two equal parts with point of stiletto, pass the silk between the divided portions of fibres, then under and back between them again, figure of eight wise, do this twice, a turn in front with two half hitches.   If these operations have been done correctly, it will be found that the fibres make a twist near the butts and fan out.   This fanning out is caused by the silk when passed figure of eight wise, between the divided portions of the hackle fibres, drawing and pressing them against the turn of silk at the back of them.   The fibres of each wing should stand out on each side like a Chinese fan, at an angle of about 45 degrees to each other.

They can then be trimmed to the shape of the natural fly's wings.

The leg hackle is now tied in by the stem in front of the wings, brought round and under to the back of them where two turns are made, it is then brought between the wings to the front where two or more turns are made, depending on the length of the hackle.   Finish off with whip finish.

Spent Drake with Split Hackle Horizontal Wings

HOOK.   Long-shanked Mayfly, Nos. 5 or 6 (Veniard's Nos. 9 or 10).

SILK.   White or pale flesh coloured Nylusta (No. 1 or 9A Gossamer).

WHISKS.   Three fibres from a cock pheasants tail or six stiff dark blue game cock's hackle fibres.

BODY.   White Sisel fibre or wool fibres from a Merino sheep.

RIBBING.   Silver tinsel.

BODY HACKLE.   Light Plymouth Rock cock's.

WING HACKLE.   Large pale dun cock's, dyed medium blue.

LEGS HACKLE.   Pale Plymouth Rock cock's.

METHOD OF DRESSING

Having tied the body in the usual way up to the shoulder, the hackle for the wings which should be long in the fibre, is tied in by the stem at the shoulder and four or five turns are made with it round the shank, then fixed with two half hitches.   The hackle fibres are now worked with the fingers and thumbs so as to have an equal portion of fibres standing out horizontally on each side. The silk is now passed between the divided portions of the fibres, then round, under and back between them again, figure of eight wise, a turn of silk in front and fixed with two half hitches.   The hook is now taken from the vice and any fibres which have not been caught by the figure of eight turns of silk underneath are trimmed off close to the body and hook returned to vice.   The leg is now tied in by the stem in front of the wings, brought round and under to the back of them where two turns of the hackle are made then brought between the wings to the front where not more than two turns are made, finishing off with whip finish.

Grey Squirrel Mayfly

TYING SILK.   Pale Yellow

HOOK.   Long-shanked 9 or 10.

TAIL WHISKS.   Three fibres from a cock pheasant's tail.

BODY.   Fur from flank of grey squirrel.

RIBS.   Flat silver tinsel, or silver Lurex.

WINGS.   Fibres from grey squirrel's tail.

HACKLE.   Light Plymouth Rock (Grizzle) dyed light olive.

METHOD OF DRESSING

After having dressed the body in the usual way up to the shoulder, a pinch of hairs is cut from the squirrel tail and tied in tightly to form the wings.   Varnish-

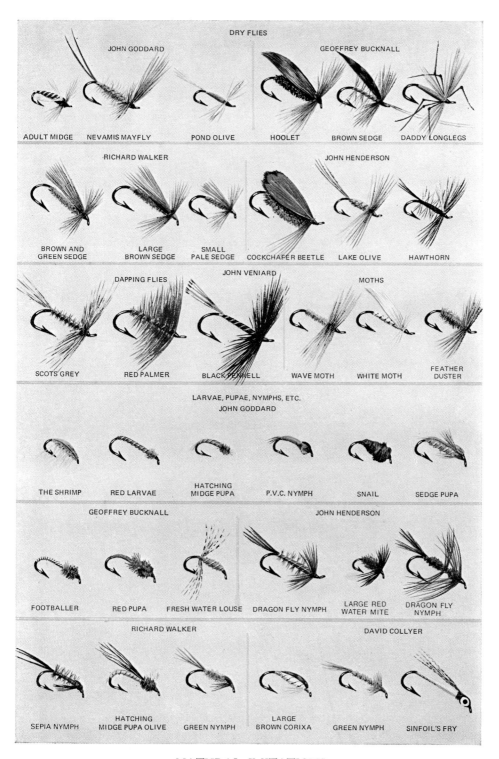

NATURAL IMITATIONS

ing at the tyings will make for more security. The wing hairs are then divided into two and fixed in an upright position with figure of eight turns of the tying silk.

The hackle is now tied in by the stem in front of the wings, brought down under and then up behind the wings where three or more turns are made as close to the wings as possible so as to keep them upright. One turn between the wings and two or more in front of them, and finish off with the whip finish.

CARIBOU FUR BODIES

Of late years this material has been used in the U.S.A. for dressing the bodies of salmon dry-flies and its success is due to its good floating qualities, Red deer's fur does equally well. These clipped fur bodied flies have also proved successful for dressing some of the larger trout flies such as Sedges and Mayflies. The following is a brief description of the method of making these clipped fur bodies:

Cut a small bunch of fur from a piece of Caribou or Red deer hide, place the bunch against the hook at bend, make two *loose* turns of the silk round the middle of the bunch and shank of hook, now pull the silk tight, this makes hairs radiate round the shank in a most surprising manner. By brushing the hairs back, the silk is brought in front of them where one turn is made and a half hitch. Another bunch of fur is laid against the shank close up to the first, the process being repeated until the shoulder is reached. When the last bunch of hair is fixed here, finish off with a whip finish and cut the silk off.

The hook is now taken from the vice and the hairs which radiate thickly round the shank, are clipped down fairly close to form a bulky Mayfly body. The hook is replaced in the vice and the silk is tied in and fixed at the end of the body near the bend if the hook. The tail is now tied in and the silk is wound spirally up body, through the clipped hairs to the shoulder, here the dressings of the wings and legs hackles is completed as described in the dressing of Green Drake and Spent Drake. The reason why the tail is not tied in until after the body is formed is because, in the trimming of the body hairs, the tail is very liable to be cut if tied in before, the same applies to the tying silk at the shoulder.

(This description of making caribou fur bodies will be more helpful if considered with my description of how to make hair bodied flies described on page 34. John V.)

THE LAKE OLIVE (*Cloeon simile*)

This fly occurs on most of our lakes but only in some of our reservoirs in the west and south of England. It is a robust fly, larger than any of the olives of our rivers, in large specimens, being about the size of a Yellow Upright, and can be distinguished from them as it has only two wings. It seems to vary considerably in colour and size, for instance, on Lough Arrow in Ireland, where it appears in May, shortly before the Mayfly hatch, the base of the wings are a grass green colour while on Blagdon, where the main hatch also occurs in May, they are a pale yellowish green in colour. The size of the fly is considerably smaller in the hatches which may take place later on in the season.

After it hatches, it remains on the surface of the water for an appreciable time and with a breeze it drifts along like a miniature sailing craft, hence it is known on Loch Leven as the "Sail Wing".

Trout seem to feed on the nymph to a greater extent than on the hatched fly and it is only when there is an extra big hatch or there is an accumulation of fly which has collected in a sheltered patch that they consider it worth while to feed on the fly at the surface.

Lake Olive

HOOK. No. 2 (13).

TYING SILK. Olive.

WHISKS. Five fibres from a dun cock's spade feather.

BODY. Three grey fibres from a blue game cock's tail feather dyed light olive or three light heron herls dyed light yellow.

RIBBING. Fine gold wire or yellow silk.

HACKLES. Light dun cock's dyed light yellow followed by a medium dun cock's (undyed).

Lake Olive Nymph

HOOK. No. 2 (13).

TYING SILK. Olive.

WHISKS AND BODY. Three fibres from a blue game cock's tail, dyed light olive, the points forming the short whisks, the remainder being wound up shank to form body.

RIBBING. Fine gold wire or yellow silk.

THORAX. Dark olive seal's fur mixture.

HACKLE. Two turns of small dun hen's.

Lake Olive Spinner

HOOK. No. 2 (13).

TYING SILK. Nylusta, tan shade, (6B Gossamer).

WHISKS. Five fibres from a medium cock's spade feather.

BODY. Light fiery brown mixed with ginger seal's fur.

RIBBING. Fine gold wire.

HACKLE (WINGS).   Light dun cock's spread out horizontally.

HACKLE. (LEGS)   Medium red cock's.

The method of dressing the spinner is similar to that of the Spent Drake.

THE CLARET DUN

My first experience of this fly was on Lough Arrow, over fifty years ago. Here there was nearly always a good hatch in certain parts of the lough in the month of May, shortly before the Mayfly hatch started.   When in sufficient numbers they were taken well by the trout.

Now Lough Arrow is one of the limestone lakes of Ireland and its waters being highly alkaline should not be suitable for the Claret Dun as they are known to prefer living in neutral or acid water.   However, several parts of the shores of the lough are peaty, which, where they occur, may produce sufficient acid in the water to suit them.

I have also observed them on many of the lakes in Snowdonia, and fairly recently while on a visit to Tal-ly-lyn (Llyn Mwyngill) during the month of May, found there were hatches of both Lake Olives and Claret Duns about mid-day.   I rather expected the trout to have a preference for the darker fly such as happens on a river when there are hatches of Olives and Iron Blues at the same time, however, the trout did not seem to have any preference for one or the other as autopsies showed about an equal quantity of each fly.

For some years now, the Claret Dun has been colonising the Birmingham Corporation's reservoirs in the Elan valley in Radnorshire, and it is satisfactory to note an increase in their numbers in recent years.   The general impression one has of the fly is that it is about the same size as a Large Dark Olive, has three setae, its wings are of a very dark greyish brown, the body and legs dark sepia, the setae greyish brown.

The spinner has almost transparent wings with body a very dark claret and legs sepia.   The setae are of a light spangled brown.

Claret Dun

HOOK.   No. 2 (13).

TYING SILK.   Dark claret.

WHISKS.   Five dark fibres from a rusty dun cock's spade feather.

BODY.   Very dark claret seal's fur.

RIBBING.   Fine gold wire.

HACKLE.   Very dark rusty dun cock's.

Nymph

HOOK.   No. 2 (13).

TYING SILK.   Dark claret.

WHISKS AND BODY.   Three fibres from a cock pheasant's tail, dyed dark claret the points forming the whisks (short), the remainder are wound up shank to shoulder to form body.

RIBBING.   Fine gold wire.

THORAX.   Very dark claret seal's fur.

HACKLE.   Two turns of dark dun hen's.

Spinner

HOOK.   No. 2 (13).

TYING SILK.   Dark claret or dark brown Nylusta.

WHISKS.   Five fibres from a very dark dun cock's spade feather.

BODY.   Dark claret seal's fur.

RIBBING.   Fine gold wire.

HACKLE (WINGS).   Light dun cock's, long in fibre.

HACKLE (LEGS).   Very dark dun cock's.

The method of dressing the spinner with wings spent, is similar to that of the Spent Drake.

CAENIDAE (Broadwings)

There are several species in this genus but only one or two are large enough to be successfully imitated by the fly-dresser such as C. horaria and C. robusta, the rest being too minute to do so.

When I lived on the banks of the Usk, I often went down to the river in the early mornings before the sun rose above the valley, as I found this the most likely time to catch a salmon.   Quite frequently when I reached the river on these early morning visits, I found the surface covered with spinners of one of the smaller Caenidae with clouds of them still dropping on the water.   Needless to say, every trout was at the surface feeding on them, but as these smaller species were so minute, I never attempted to tie a fly to represent them.

Two of the larger species occur on some lakes and reservoirs from May to September and when conditions are favourable, hatch in enormous numbers just as it is getting dark.   In newly constructed reservoirs they establish themselves surprisingly quickly although not so quickly as Chironomids.

By far the best description of these flies is given in *Lake Flies and their Imitations* by C. F. Walker who has given them the name of Broadwings as they have abnormally broad wings, another distinguishing feature is that they have three tails.

As in the case of other water flies which sometimes hatch in enormous numbers such as March Browns, Iron Blues and Chironomids, the nymph is more effective in catching trout than the dry-fly. This is particularly so as regards "Broadwings" as they usually hatch when the light is failing fast and it becomes impossible to see ones fly or distinguish it from the thousands surrounding it.

The larger species of the Caenis are about the same size as a small P.W.D. but their bodies are more plump, so a P.W.D. dressed on a No. oo hook with a plump body should be sufficiently like the fly when it hatches, but the trout will be feeding almost entirely on the nymph as it rises to the surface and particularly as its body hangs vertically below the surface before hatching.

We have now to consider the dressings of the nymph and the spinner of these larger species which I now give:

Dressing of Caenis Nymph

HOOK.   No. oo (16).

SILK.   Light flesh coloured Nylusta, (3 or 9A Gossamer).

WHISKS.   Four or five short fibres from a white cocks hackle.

BODY.   Natural ostrich herl (pale stone colour).

RIBBING.   Thin gold wire.

THORAX.   Several turns of bronze peacock herl or dark brown polymer dubbing.

Dressing of Caenis Spinner

HOOK.   No. oo (16).

SILK.   Light flesh coloured Nylusta, (3 or 9A Gossamer).

WHISK.   Four or five long fibres from a white cock's hackle.

BODY.   Fibre from a white swan's feather, dyed cream.

RIBBING.   Light flesh coloured Nylusta.

WINGS.   White cock's hackle spread out horizontally and trimmed to shape and size.

LEGS.   Light stone coloured ostrich herl, two turns behind the wings, one turn between the wings and two turns in front of wings. The details of dressing split hackle horizontal wings will be found under Spent Drake, page 80.

WILLOW FLY (*Leuctra genticulata*)

This is essentially an autumn fly and does not appear in any numbers until September, mostly on upland reservoirs, where on a day of sun and cloud, whenever there is a burst of sunshine, they may appear in large numbers.

The length of the body of the fly is about $\frac{3}{8}$-inch, the wings when closed extend behind the body by about $\frac{1}{8}$-inch. The colour of the thorax and legs, is a dark olive but the body shades off to a golden yellow towards the tail.

Dressing

HOOK.   No. 1 or 2 (14 or 18).

BODY.   Seal's fur, shading from golden yellow at tail to dark olive at shoulder.

HACKLE (BODY).   Medium dun cock's trimmed a little if necessary, tied in by stem at shoulder and wound down body to bend where the tip of the hackle is bound on top of shank by the ribbing (fine gold wire) which is then wound up body to shoulder.

HACKLE (SHOULDER).   Medium dun cock's.

The hackle point left at the tail can be shortened and rounded so as to represens the folded wings of the natural fly which extend beyond the body.

The Daddy-long-legs

HOOK.   Long May Fly No. 5 (10).

BODY AND LEGS.   Four fibres from a peacock's wing feather, about two inch long.

RIBBING.   Fine gold tinsel.

WINGS.   Mottled cock's hackle points.

HACKLE (FOR FLOTATION ONLY).   A light dun or ginger cock's hackle.

METHOD OF DRESSING

The four fibres from the peacock's wing feather, which is of a light fawn colour, are knotted about $\frac{3}{4}$-inch from the tips to represent the leg joints, and are then tied in by their butts together with the ribbing at the bend of the hook, the tying silk is wound up the shank to the shoulder and fixed with a half hitch. The hook is then taken from the vice and replaced up-side down, so that the point of the hook is above the shank. The four fibres are now turned up the shank to the shoulder, not twisted together before doing so, but spread out at much as possible while making the turns. About four turns will bring them to the shoulder, where they are held vertically and fixed in this position by the tying silk. They should be about $1\frac{1}{2}$-inch long, which is about the right length for the legs. The fibres are now separated, two on each side and the tying silk brought figure-of-eight wise between them, this is followed by at least two turns between the pair of legs on each side. The ribbing is now wound up body, through the legs and finished off beyond them. The hook is now taken from the vice and replaced in normal position. The two mottled hackle points for the wings are now tied in at the shoulder, are separated by the tying silk, figure-of-eight wise between them, they should slope somewhat towards the tail end. The hackle is tied in by the stem in front of the wings, then brought down, under and behind the wings where at least four turns are made, then one turn between the wings and three or more in front of them, depending on the length of the hackle. Finish off with whip finish.

THE NON-BITING MIDGES (*Chironomids*)

Throughout the year from March to October there is a continual hatch of these flies. Only a few of them are large enough to be of use to the fly-fisher and of these I am describing four, namely (1) The Olive Midge, (2) The Black Midge. (3) The Green Midge, (4) The Light Grey Midge.

(1) THE OLIVE MIDGE (*Chironomus plumosus*)

Besides C. plumosus it can also be taken to include several species very similar in appearance, as according to F. W. Edwards, C. plumosus is not very clearly defined from several other species of the group among them being C. dorsalis which was selected by Miall and Hammond, on account of its size and abundance nearly all the year round, as the most suitable example of the Chironomidae for examination. They have described it in great detail in their book *The Structure and Life History of the Harlequin Fly* (*Chironomus*). The Olive Midge is the largest of the Chironomids, being at least ½-inch in length. The males have plumed antennae and long slender bodies. The females have unplumed antennae and much stouter bodies with small milky coloured wings which seem almost too small to carry such a bulky body. The colour of the body is usually a dark greyish olive. It seems to prefer lakes and reservoirs which are alkaline and not too deep. It is common on Blagdon Lake where it is known as the Blagdon Buzzer, hatching out in great numbers during the early summer. The trout seem to prefer taking the hatching nymph to the fly.

DRESSING OF THE OLIVE MIDGE

Mosely's dressing as given in *The Field* of September 9th, 1911. Hook, 1 to 3; Body, dark olive condor quill, unstripped; Legs, a very green olive hackle; Wings, two short blue hackle points set along the body; Thorax, a few fibres of heron or any greyish-blue feather, tied in at the shoulder and humped over to the neck of the hook, where they should be fastened in and the fly finished off.

I have not found any dry-fly dressings of this fly very successful but I now give another dressing:

HOOK. No. 1 to 3, (14-12)
SILK. Olive
BODY. Heron herl, dyed a light brownish olive.
RIBBING. Fine gold wire.
HACKLE. Medium blue dun cock's, rather long in fibre.
WINGS. Two light dun hackle points.

Having made the body, the hackle points are tied in at the shoulder to form the wings, spread these apart and wind the silk figure-of-eight wise between them so that they are about an angle of 45 degrees to each other. Now tie in the hackle by the stem in front of the wings, bring it down under and behind the wings, make two turns behind them, one turn between them and two or more in front of them. Finish off with whip finish. The hackle should be sufficiently long in the fibre to give the fly a "variant" look.

A large Dark Olive "Variant" on a No. 2 hook makes a fairly good representation of the natural fly and if the above dressings are not available, is a fairly satisfactory alternative.

Dressing of the Olive Midge Nymph
Mr. A. S. Newsom's dressing as given in his article "Blagdon from the Bank" which appeared in the autumn 1955 *Journal* of the Flyfishers' Club:—
HOOK. No. 10 or 12.
SILK. Black.
BODY. Black floss silk wound on so as to make a slightly tapering body and carried a short way round the bend of the hook.
RIBBING. Four turns of flat gold tinsel (size 2).
ANTENNAE ("HOUSING"). White floss silk tied in at the head and cut off short.

(2) THE BLACK MIDGE (*Chironomus tentans*)

This fly is slightly smaller than the Olive Midge, reaching ½-inch in length. Its larva, the well known blood worm, lives in tube like tunnels in the mud at the bottom of lakes and reservoirs. The nymph or pupa is of a dark greyish colour and about ½-inch long. Shortly before it rises to the surface to hatch, a layer of air gas is or formed between the body and the thin transparent outer skin which gives it a silvery appearance. Although the fly may be seen during every month of the fishing season, its main hatching times are through the month of April and again towards the end of July and beginning of August. The hatches during the summer months usually take place at dusk when the fly on the surface seem to be completely ignored by trout which only feed on the nymphs which are hanging vertically from the surface, with their shoulders just through the surface film, preparatory to emerging. There may be several hundred hatching to the square yard so the odds on catching a trout are considerably against the angler, even if he is fishing with a nymph.

Dressing of the Black Midge
HOOK. No. 1 or 2 (14-13)
SILK. Dark claret or black.
BODY. Two sooty black fibres from a turkey's tail feather.

BODY HACKLE. Black cock's trimmed from $\frac{1}{4}$-inch to $\frac{1}{8}$-inch.

RIBBING: Thin gold wire or Nylex (Gun metal shade).

WINGS. Two light grey cock hackle points.

LEG HACKLE. Black hackle, untrimmed.

METHOD OF DRESSING

The two sooty black fibres together with the ribbing having been tied in at the bend, the fibres are wound up shank to the shoulder and fixed. The trimmed body hackle is now tied at the shoulder by the stem wound down the body to the bend so that the point of the hackle is all that is left. This is fixed in position on top of hook with two turns of the ribbing which is then wound up body to shoulder and fixed. The two hackle points for the wings are now tied in at the shoulder and then spread out by winding tying silk figure-of-eight wise between them so that they are about 90 degrees to each other. Now tie in the cock's hackle for the legs, by the stem in front of the wings, bring it down under and then up behind the swings, make two turns behind the wings, one turn between the wings to the front of them where two or more turns are made. Finish off with whip finish.

Dressing of the Black Midge Nymph

HOOK. No. 1 or 2 (14-13)

TYING SILK. Mulberry or Claret.

BODY. Two fibres from a Heron's wing feather, wound on from bend to shoulder.

RIBBING. Mulberry or Claret silk.

THORAX. Mole's fur.

HACKLE. Small dark dun hen's, two turns only.

Dressing No. 2

HOOK. No. 1 or 2 (14-13)

TYING SILK. Mulberry or Claret.

WHISK. Tag of Claret floss silk, cut short.

BODY. Medium red floss silk.

RIBBING Flat silver tinsel, wound on so as to leave a slight gap between the turns to show the red floss silk.

THORAX. Mole's fur.

HACKLE. Small dark dun hen's, two turns only.

(3) THE GREEN MIDGE (*Chironomus viridis*)

This fly is almost the same size as the Black Midge, that is about $\frac{1}{2}$-inch in length and similar in shape but of a pale emerald colour the wings are translucent but appear to be milky in colour.

It seems to prefer alkaline to neutral or acid waters. It does not appear to be in any numbers in the Welsh reservoirs but is common in the great limestone loughs of Ireland, also in Loch Leven in Scotland and on Blagdon Lake in Somerset. The larva is not blood red in colour but of a pale yellowish-olive and it is probable that the lack of haemoglobin in its blood prevents it living at any great depth as in the case of the larva (blood worm) of the Black Midge, it is therefore to be found in waters of no great depth. In Halford's *Dry-fly Man's Handbook*, H. T. Sheringham describes this fly and how he fished with an imitation of it on Blagdon Lake, while Richard E. Threlfall, in his book *On a Gentle Art* gives a most entertaining and interesting account of his dry-fly fishing with this fly, for large trout, in the sheltered shallow bays on the west shore of Lough Mask.

Dressing of the Green Midge

HOOK. No. 1 or 2 (14-13)
BODY. Two fibres from a swan's feather, dyed a light emerald green.
RIBBING. Thin gold wire.
WINGS. Two light grey cock hackle points.
LEGS. Light grey or very light Plymouth Rock cock's hackle. Method of dressing similar to that of the Black Midge.

Dressing of the Green Midge Nymph

HOOK. No. 1 (14)
SILK. Light olive green.
WHISK. Tag of medium green floss silk or Polymer dubbing cut short.
BODY. Medium green Polymer dubbing.
RIBBING. Flat silver tinsel wound on so as to show the green dubbing between them.
THORAX. Medium olive Polymer dubbing.
HACKLE. Light dun hen, two turns only.

THE GREY MIDGE   (*C. F. Walker's Phantom Midge*)

Quantities of this midge can be observed on Weir Wood reservoir through the summer months. It is smaller than the Black Midge and although it appears to be a light grey colour when seen on the water, if examined it will be seen that the body, being almost translucent, has a light tinge of pale green and blue in places. The trout take them well and from autopsies they seem to feed mainly on the nymphs as they are hatching at the surface.

Dressing of the Grey Midge

HOOK. No. 0 or 00 (15-16).
TYING SILK. White or light grey.

BODY. A light grey fibre from a blue game cock's tail feather or from any suitable light grey feather.

RIBBING. Pale green silk (Eau de Nil).

BODY HACKLE. Small light dun cock's trimmed from $\frac{1}{8}$-inch to $\frac{1}{16}$-inch, tied in by the stem at the shoulder and wound down body to tail, fixed with ribbing which is wound up body through hackle to shoulder.

SHOULDER HACKLE. Small light grey cock's.

Dressing of Light Grey Midge (*Phantom Midge*)

Using deer body hair for legs and wings.

HOOK. No. 0 or 00 (15-16).

TYING SILK. Flesh coloured Nylusta or nearest Gossamer tying silk, (No. 3, 10 or 9A).

BODY. Very pale green floss silk.

RIBBING. Very fine nylon monofilament wound close together up body to shoulder.

WINGS AND LEGS. A small bunch of deer body hair, almost white in colour tied in and formed as described on page 90. In this instance, however, the hairs are not cut close to the hook shank but cut to form a "hackle" and legs about $\frac{1}{3}$-inch in diameter.

Dressing of Grey Midge Nymph

HOOK. No. 0 (15).

TYING SILK. Nylusta, grey.

BODY. Light grey fibre from any suitable light grey feather.

RIBBING. Fine silver tinsel with green silk wound up body together.

THORAX. Natural ostrich herl (stone colour) two or more turns.

Note:—In *Lake Flies and their Imitation* by C. F. Walker, he describes a fly very similar to the above which he has had identified as Chaoborus crystallinus. Owing to its almost transparent body he gives it the name "Phantom Midge" which is most appropriate.

THE BLACK HACKLED DRY-FLY (*Black Palmer*)

This I consider to be the most useful all-round dry-fly on reservoirs as it not only represents the Black Midge but many other insects such as beetles and Black Silver Horn sedges.

Dressing

HOOK. No. 0 (15).

TYING SILK. Dark Claret or black.

BODY. Black ostrich or three fibres from a Magpie's tail.

RIBBING.   Thin gold wire or Nylusta (Dark grey).

BODY HACKLE.   Black cock's trimmed to taper from $\frac{1}{4}$-inch to $\frac{1}{8}$-inch.

SHOULDER HACKLE.   Black cock's untrimmed.

METHOD OF DRESSING

Tying silk is wound down body to bend.   At bend tie in ribbing of gold wire or Nylusta and the ostrich herl or magpie's tail fibres, then wind tying silk back to shoulder, the fibres to form the body are wound up body to shoulder and tied in.   The trimmed body hackle is now tied in at shoulder and wound down the body to bend and regulated so that the point of the hackle is all that is left.   This is fixed in position on top and at end of body with two turns of ribbing which is then wound up body through hackle to shoulder and tied in, the point of the hackle can be left at the tail end to form a tag.   The untrimmed cock's hackle of suitable size is now tied in by the stem at the shoulder and wound down the shank and into the body hackle for two or three turns, then back towards the eye several turns, depending on the length of the hackle.   Finish off with whip finish.

A Black Palmer dry-fly, dressed in the same way as the above but on much larger hooks such as a Wilson dry-fly salmon hook, Size 9 ($\frac{7}{8}$-inch) are used on Loch Maree for sea trout.

THE HAWTHORN FLY (*Bibio marci*) AND THE HEATHER FLY (*Bibio pomonae*)

These two flies are near relations and of the same size and appearance particularly in flight when they both trail their long hind legs behind them, the only difference being that the Hawthorn Fly is all black while the Heather Fly is all black except the femurs of the legs which are a bright red colour.   The Hawthorn Fly makes its appearance in May and early June and the Heather Fly in August and September.

Dressing

HOOK.   No. 3 (12).

TYING SILK.   Black.

BODY.   Black Polymer dubbing.

RIBBING.   Thin gold wire.

BODY HACKLE.   Black cock's, trimmed from $\frac{1}{4}$-inch to $\frac{1}{8}$-inch.

WINGS.   Two light grey hackle points.

SHOULDER HACKLE.   Black cock's for Hawthorn Fly and a dark Cochy-
    bonddu cock's for Heather Fly.

METHOD OF DRESSING

Tie in ribbing at bend of hook and dub the body with black Polymer dubbing tie the trimmed cock's hackle by the stem at the shoulder and wind it down the body to bend, regulating the winding, so that on reaching the tail end of the body, only the point of hackle remains, this is fixed by a turn of the ribbing on top of the hook, the ribbing being now wound up body through the body hackle to shoulder. Now tie in the light grey hackle points, at shoulder, to form the wings, separate them and pass the tying silk figure-of-eight wise between them and make two half hitches in front of them. Tie in the shoulder hackle (black for Hawthorn Fly and Cochybonddu for Heather Fly) by the stem in front of wings, bring it down under and behind the wings, make two or three turns behind the wings, one turn between the wings, two or more in front of them and finish off with whip finish.

Hackle pattern:—Proceed as above for body and body hackle. For Hawthorn Fly, tie in black shoulder hackle followed by a Plymouth Rock hackle. For the Heather Fly tie in a rich red Cochybonddu shoulder hackle followed by a Pymouth Rock hackle.

THE ALDER (sialis lutaria)

This fly is to be seen along the shores of most reservoirs from the middle of May to the middle of June. The female fly is considerably larger and more bulky than the male, being about $\frac{3}{4}$-inch long whereas the male is only about $\frac{1}{2}$-inch long. As the natural fly when on the surface of the water is usually fluttering, the hackle pattern is the most practical to use.

Dressing of Fly

HOOK. For male No. 1 or 2, for female No. 3 or 4 (14 to 11).

TYING SILK. Brown Nylusta (No. 17 Gossamer).

BODY. Five fibres a cock pheasant's tail feather, tied in by the butts at the bend of hook, the tag ends being bound firmly along the top of the shank. The five fibres are now twisted together and wound up to shoulder to form body.

RIBBING. Brown Nylusta.

BODY HACKLE. Rusty dun cock's, trimmed from $\frac{1}{2}$-inch to $\frac{1}{4}$-inch, tied in by the stem at shoulder and wound down body to bend so that only the tip of the hackle remains, this is fixed on the top of the shank by two turns of the ribbing which is then wound up body to shoulder and fixed with two half hitches.

WING HACKLE. A dark brown, slightly speckled feather from the back of a mallard, or a dark brown mottled feather from the breast of an old cock grouse, this is tied in by the stem in front of the body hackle and given the necessary turns and finish off with whip finish.

Note:—With regard to the fibres from a cock pheasant's tail feather, if the reverse side of a tail feather is examined, it will be noted that a considerable portion of the fibres from the mid-rib outwards are black or heavily mottled with black, the remaining portions of the fibres to their tips being a reddish brown, hence the reason for tying in the fibres by the butts for the blackish brown body of the Alder and by the points for the reddish brown body of the P.T.

Dressing of the Winged Pattern

BODY AND BODY HACKLE similar to hackle pattern.

WINGS. The marginal covert feathers from the wings of a blue game cock or hen. These feathers are to be found on the edge of the wing close to the wrist joint. They have very strong mid-ribs and one margin is more convex than the other. Select a feather from the right wing and another from the left wing to match it. Tie one on each side of the shoulder so that the convex edges are uppermost and come flush together over the body, pent house fashion. In order to do this satisfactorily, it will be found necessary to trim the tops of the body hackle fibres.

HEAD HACKLE. A dark rusty dun cock's hackle, about four turns in front of the wings, finishing off with whip finish.

A fly so dressed makes a very realistic imitation of the natural fly, giving it the characteristic hump-backed shape. However, it requires much practice to set the wings properly and it does not stand up to wear so well as the hackle pattern.

THE SEDGES

For the dry-fly man, the day flying sedges are the most satisfactory as their imitation can be fished in daylight and not in the poor light of the evenings when most of the other sedges make their appearance, by which time the failing light soon makes it too dark to see his fly. There are not many of these day flying sedges on reservoirs and lakes, but the most noticeable among them are the Black and Brown Silverhorns, although they do not usually come out in any numbers until the late afternoon. Another small day-flying sedge of a light brown colour (*Tinodes waeneri*) can often be seen round the shores in fair numbers. On Lough Arrow, in Ireland, during the early summer, it sometimes appears in enormous numbers. The Welshman's Button is a day flying sedge and although there were fair numbers on Lough Arrow during the Mayfly season, as happens on most of our chalk streams, I have only seen an occasional one on the reservoirs and lakes in England and Wales.

However, I include it in my list as the artificial does to represent several other brown sedges which make their appearance during the evenings. Of the evening sedges, the Cinnamon sedges (*Limnophilidae*) are the most common. I give a general dressing for the medium sized evening sedges which does to represent the Cinnamon sedges as well as several others of the same colour but smaller such as Molanna Angustata.

The biggest of our sedges is the Large Red Sedge (*Phrygania grandis*), it is $\frac{3}{4}$-inch long with a wing span of 2 inches. I give a dressing of this fly which has accounted for a number of fish. But one of the most satisfactory evenings fishing I had when these great flies were scuttering about on the surface, was at Blagdon, when not finding a big enough sedge in my fly-box, I put on a fly which I had dressed some years previously to represent a Cockchafer (see dressing under Beetles), and with it I caught two nice trout before it got too dark to see anything.

It may be only coincidence that during the last century, the best imitation for the brown day flying sedge (*Seristoma personatum*), of the chalk streams, was a fly originally dressed to imitate a beetle called the Welshman's Button, also known as Marlow Buzz or Cochybonddu beetle.

DETAILS OF THE DRESSINGS

Dressing of the Black Silverhorns
HOOK. No. 0 (15).
TYING SILK. Nylusta (Gunmetal), (No. 10 Gossamer).
BODY. Black Polymer dubbing or three fibres from a Magpie's tail.
RIBBING. Pale green Gossamer thread (Coat's Terylene Y639).
BODY HACKLE. Black cock's trimmed to taper from $\frac{1}{4}$-inch to $\frac{1}{16}$-inch.
SHOULDER HACKLE. Black hen's or a small feather from a black hen's breast.

Dressing of the Brown Silverhorns
HOOK. No. 0.
TYING SILK. Nylusta (Medium brown).
BODY. Dark green Polymer or seal's dubbing mixed with hare's ear.
RIBBING. Nylusta (Gunmetal shade). (No. 10 Gossamer).
BODY HACKLE. Rusty dun cock's trimmed from $\frac{1}{4}$-inch to $\frac{1}{16}$-inch.
SHOULDER HACKLE. Wood cock's neck or Landrail's feather from wing.

The method of dressing for both the above is the same as for the "Black Hackle Dry-fly". The dressing of the light brown sedge (*Tinodes waeneri*) is the same as for the Brown Silverhorn, but with a light brown body.

Dressing of Weishman's Button (*Sericostoma personatum*)

HOOK. No. 3.

TYING SILK. Nylusta (Chestnut), (No. 17 Gossamer).

BODY. Four fibres from a cock pheasant's tail, tied in by the butts at the bend, and wound up body to shoulder.

RIBBING. Fine gold tinsel.

BODY HACKLE. Dark rusty dun cock's, trimmed to taper from $\frac{5}{8}$-inch to $\frac{1}{4}$-inch. Tied in at the shoulder by stem and wound down body to bend. Fix point of hackle by a turn of the ribbing which is then wound up body to shoulder and tied in.

SHOULDER HACKLE. Cock Copper Pheasant's breast feather, fibres about $\frac{3}{4}$-inch long. Rhode Island Red breast feather or that of a cross between a Rhode Island and a Sussex will do as well.

Dressing of the Cinnamon Sedges (*Limnophilidae*)

HOOK. No. 3 or 4 (12-11).

TYING SILK. Nylusta, light brown, (No. 6B Gossamer).

BODY. Light yellowish brown seal's fur mixture for males, green seal's fur dubbing for females of L. lunatus.

RIBBING. Fine gold tinsel.

BODY HACKLE. Light red or ginger cock's.

SHOULDER HACKLES. Light red cock's followed by a light brown feather from a brown hen's breast.

Dressing of the Large Red Sedge

HOOK. No. 6 new No. 9, Old Redditch scale.

TYING SILK Nylusta, brown, (No. 17 Gossamer).

BODY. Yellowish brown seal's fur mixture.

RIBBING. Gold tinsel.

BODY HACKLE. Red cock's.

SHOULDER HACKLES. Red cock's followed by a Rhode Island hen's hackle or a feather from the breast of a Rhode Island cock or hen.

Also the dressing I have given for the Cockchafer, No. 2, with thick Condor fibre body, ginger hackle, with two feathers from the breast of a cock pheasant, tied one on top of the other, so as to rest along the top of the body.

Dressing of Cinnamon Sedge Nymph

HOOK. Nos. 2 or 3 (13-12).

TYING SILK. Nylusta, brown, (No. 17 Gossamer).

BODY. Seal's fur mixture of dirty orange and brown.

RIBBING. Fine gold tinsel.

HACKLE. Long fibred light red cock's, two turns.

WING CASES. Two short lengths of black ostrich herl, $\frac{3}{16}$-inch long tied in at shoulder so as to lie as flat as possible on body.

Beetles

THE COCKCHAFER (*Melolontha melolontha*)

This, is one of our largest beetles, being from 1-inch to $1\frac{1}{8}$-inch in length and $\frac{1}{2}$-inch in width. Its wing cases and legs are a reddish brown and the under-parts of its body banded black and grey. It makes its appearance from the middle of May to the middle of June. In some years they may occur in great numbers but this can be followed by an interval of many years when few are seen. As in the case of most beetles, the Cockchafer, when it pitches on the surface of the water, is unable to fold its wings under the wing cases and they remain unfolded and projecting beyond the end of the body. This tendency of floating beetles to have their wings trailing beyond the end of the body is of some practical use to the dry-fly fisherman as it enables him to dress his imitation with a feathered projection at the tail which helps to hold the fly up on the surface and improve its floatation.

I have experimented with three different dressings:
(1) With cork body.
(2) With Condor fibre body.
(3) With Caribou fur body.

(1) Dressing with Cork Body

HOOK. Long May No. 7 to 8.

SILK. Nylusta, brown, (No. 17 Gossamer).

TAIL. Two light dun cock hackle points $\frac{3}{4}$-inch long.

BODY. Cork, oval shape with flat underside, about 1-inch and $\frac{1}{2}$-inch wide. A groove is cut with a fine saw down the centre of the body about $\frac{1}{16}$-inch deep this is filled with "Durofix" or "Bostick". The shank of the hook is now pressed down into the groves so that the tail end of the cork body is at the bend of the hook and leaving sufficient room at the head for tying on the hackle and wing cases. It is then left to dry for some hours and then painted a dark grey all over and if one wishes to be very exact in the imitation, thin white bands can be painted on the underside.

HACKLE. Large red cock's.

WING CASES. Two brownish-red heart-shaped feathers with black edges from a cock pheasant's breast, place one on top of the other, tie by stems close up to the hackle, so that they extend down the back of the body and finish off.

(2) Dressing with Condor Herl Body

HOOK, SILK AND TAIL similar dressing (1).

BODY. Tie in seven or eight dark grey Condor fibres at bend of hook leaving about ½-inch of the tags of the Condor fibres to be tied in firmly along the top of the shank and fixed with "Cellire" varnish. Now take all the Condor fibres in the hackle pliers and wind them round the shank and over the tied in tag ends, towards the head, so as to make the body as bulky as possible.

RIBBING. Fine gold tinsel which was tied in with tail.

BODY HACKLE. A large red cock's, tied in at shoulder and wound down body through hackle to shoulder and fixed with two half hitches.

WING CASES. Two feathers from a cock pheasant's breast and tied in as described in Dressing No. 1.

(3) Dressing with Caribou Fur Body

HOOK, SILK AND TAIL. similar to dressing No. 1.

BODY. Caribou fur trimmed to size of body of the natural insect, that is, about 1-inch long and ½-inch in diameter.

SHOULDER HACKLE AND WING CASES, similar to dressing Nos. 1 and 2.

I consider this to be the most satisfactory dressing for a Cockchafer as the trimmed Caribou fur makes a body sufficiently bulky and it floats well.

When tying No. 3 dressing I found that the most satisfactory hook for the purpose was the Wilson dry-fly salmon hook (sizes No. 10 and 12), as it is much wider in the gape than the Long May hooks. With such a bulky body as the Cockchafer, a wide gape is essential.

(Details for dressing Caribou fur body, see page 81).

THE COCHYBONDDU BEETLE (*Phyllopertha horticola*)

This beetle has been given various names; Ronalds calls it the Marlow Buzz and it is also known as the Hazel Fly, Shorn Fly and the June Bug. It is about ½-inch long, the thorax, head, underparts and legs being a dark shiny green and the wing cases a bright reddish brown. It begins to appear about the end of May and continues to the end of June. On a sunny afternoon in June, on a reservoir in the Welsh mountains, I have seen the surface of the water, which a few moments before, was void of all insects and no fish rising, suddenly become agitated with rising fish and the surface speckled with quantities of the beetles. This queer urge to shift their quarters does not usually take place before noon and the usual time to expect it is from then to about 2 p.m. they seem to require a certain amount of sun and warmth for them to take wing. On a dull wet day they remain roosting in the foliage.

HOOK. No. 1 or 2 (14-13).

TYING SILK. Nylusta (brown), (No. 17 Gossamer)

RIBBING. Fine gold tinsel.

BODY. Five or six peacock herls twisted together and wound up body to shoulder.

BODY HACKLE. A black cock's trimmed from $\frac{1}{4}$-inch to $\frac{1}{8}$-inch, tied in by the stem at the shoulder and wound down body to bend where it is fixed on top of shank by the ribbing, leaving the point of the hackle (which should be at least $\frac{1}{4}$-inch long) as a tail, the ribbing is then wound up body to shoulder and fixed by tying silk.

SHOULDER HACKLE. A bright reddish brown Cochybonddu hackle, tied in at shoulder immediately above the body hackle, take two or three turns into the body hackle and then back towards the eye, at least six turns in all. Finish off with whip finish.

SOME OTHER SMALL BEETLES

Most of those found in autopsies are either black for "Staphs", dark brown for "Skipjacks" or in the case of some of the weevils, a brownish-grey. The most useful fly to represent most of these small dark beetles is the Black Palmer on hook No. 0, (15).

I now give two further dressings which should cover most types of these smaller beetles.

Dressing A

HOOK. No. 0 to 2 (15-13).

SILK. Nylusta (Gunmetal shade). (No. 10 Gossamer).

BODY. Peacock herl, black Ostrich herl or three fibres from a Magpie's tail.

BODY HACKLE. Black cock's trimmed from $\frac{1}{8}$-inch to $\frac{1}{16}$-inch.

SHOULDER HACKLE. Black or dark rusty dun cock's, untrimmed.

Dressing B

HOOK. Nos. 0 to 1 (15-14).

SILK. Nylusta (Gunmetal shade).

BODY. Condor herl.

BODY HACKLE. Medium dun cock's, trimmed from $\frac{1}{8}$-inch to $\frac{1}{16}$-inch.

SHOULDER HACKLE. Medium dun cock's, untrimmed.

Note. The Ribbing in both these dressings is thin gold wire or Nylusta (Gunmetal).

CORIXIDAE

I have not found these in autopsies of trout from any of the "Upland" reservoirs, and it was not until I commenced to fish on Blagdon, some thirty years ago, that I noticed them in autopsies. The Corixids lay their eggs here in large gelatinous masses attached to water-weeds. These hatch out into nymphs which gradually grow in size until they finally change from the nymph to the adult insect which is about $\frac{1}{2}$-inch in length, can fly as well as being an expert swimmer, hence its popular name of the "Water Boatman". Trout feed on them during the egg stage, through the nymph stage and finally on the adult insect. The gelatinous masses containing the eggs are of a yellow, almost orange colour, and on several occasions, while fishing on Blagdon Lake, I have found portions of this gelatinous mass attached to pieces of weed in autopsies of trout as well as a quantity of nymphs and some adults.

There seems little doubt that trout browse among the weeds and when they see a yellow mass containing the eggs attached to the weeds, they gulp it in weed and all.

An angler I met at Blagdon fished mainly with an imitation of the Corixa nymph, about $\frac{1}{4}$-inch long, which he dressed himself on a No. 1 hook, the body being loaded slightly and dubbed with Rabbit or hare's fur, with about two turns of brown partridge hackle at shoulder. The gut seemed to me to be on the thin side for Blagdon, being not thicker than .22 mm, however I gathered he caught a number of trout on this fine tackle.

It is not only trout who consider Corixa eggs a delicacy, for according to L. C. Miall, in his book *The Natural History of Aquatic Insects*, he says; "these masses of Corixa eggs have served as an article of food to the Mexicans. They are gathered in the lakes of Chalco and Texcuco which adjoin the city of Mexico. Reeds are set in bundles in the shallows of the lakes and upon these the "Water Boatman" lay their eggs which are gathered and detached by beating. They are made into cakes with meal and are said to have an agreeable acid taste".

Dressing for Corixa
No. (1). A suggestion to imitate an egg mass attached to weeds

HOOK. Nos. 4 or 5 (11-10).

SILK. Green.

BODY.   Green Polymer dubbing to represent a stock of weed.

RIBBING.   Gold tinsel.

HACKLE.   A white fluffy feather, dyed yellow, which should almost veil the body, in much the same manner as the fluffy feather does in the Grey Eagle salmon fly.

No. (2) Corixa nymph

HOOK.   Nos. 1 or 2 (14-13).

SILK.   Nylusta, brown.

BODY.   Loaded slightly with fine copper wire which is covered with a mixture of hare's fur (stone colour).

RIBBING.   Fine gold tinsel.

SHOULDER HACKLE.   Two turns of a small partridge feather (brown).

No. (3) Corixa, adult

HOOK.   No. 3 (12).

SILK.   Nylusta brown, (No 17 Gossamer).

BODY.   Loaded slightly with fine copper wire which is covered with a mixture of hare's fur (stone colour).

LEGS.   Before the body is made, two centre-ribs of a feather, not too stiff, the fibres having been trimmed down close to the mid-rib. These are tied in half way down the shank so as to stand out at about 60 degrees to the lower part of the body, the length being about $\frac{1}{2}$-inch.

SHOULDER HACKLE.   Two turns of a small feather from a wood cock's breast.

DRAGONFLY NYMPHS AT BLAGDON

During the month of June there is generally a great hatch of Dragonflies of the thin bodied type known as Demoiselle-flies, the most numerous being the pale blues, bronzy-greens and reds. The nymphs are of a duller colour, ranging from mottled greenish-grey to dull bronzy-red.

As soon as the sun is well up, the nymphs commence their trek along the bottom and on the top of weed beds towards the shore and as soon as they reach it they crawl out and up anything from an angler's wader to rushes and reeds. When well above the surface of the water, they hatch from the nymphal skin. It is during this trek to the shore that the trout feed on them and continue to do so, underwater, even when they are climbing up the reeds before hatching. I have strong suspicions that trout occasionally take a nymph from a stationary angler's waders. Their mode of progress during the trek is a queer and characteristic motion which can only be described as a combination of swimming, wriggling and crawling.

In fishing with the artificial nymph, although it is impossible to copy the motions of the natural insect, the nearest one can do is to sink the artificial to as near the bottom as possible and draw it in by little jerks. The first experiment I made of the imitation of a dragonfly nymph were not successful in temping trout to take it, the reasons were probably that the hooks were unloaded and therefore keeping too near the surface, another reason being that the hackles used being cock's were too stiff to give the necessary movement to the legs.

I made two other dressings, (1) with floss silk bodies, some blue and red, covered with flattened Platil, which was no more successful. (2) with various bodies including peacock herl and hackled with a feather from a cock Pheasant's rump, two turns of hackle half way down the body and several turns at the head. I have not been able to test these as my last visit to Blagdon was in May which is too early for the Dragonfly hatch.

Dressing of Dragonfly Nymphs
No. 1 Dressing
HOOK. Long May, loaded with one or two layers of thin copper wire.
TYING SILK. Dark red.
BODY. Fiery brown seals fur.
RIBBING. Gold oval tinsel.
HACKLE. Rhode Island Red hen.
TAIL. Two hackle tips from a Rhode Island Red cock.

No. 2 Dressing
HOOK. Same as in Dressing No. 1.
TYING SILK. Olive.
BODY. Greyish green seal's fur mixture.
RIBBING. Gold oval tinsel.
HACKLE. Barred Plymouth Rock hen, dyed bluish-green.
TAIL. Two hackle tips from a dark Plymouth Rock cock.

No. 3 Dressing
HOOK. Same as in Dressing No. 1.
BODY. Floss silk, red covered by flattened Platil.
BODY HACKLE. Red cock hackle, clipped.
HACKLE. Rhode Island Red hen.
TAIL. Two cock's hackle tips to match colour of body.

No. 4 Dressing
HOOK. Same as in Dressing No. 1.
BODY. Bronze Peacock herl.
RIBBING. Gold tinsel.

HACKLES. Soft feather from rump of cock pheasant, two turns of hackle half way down the body and two or more turns of hackle at head.

TAIL. Tip of cock pheasant's rump feather.

FLYING ANTS

Dressing of these flies are not often needed, in fact, through the greater part of the fishing season, from say the beginning of the season to the end of July one need not bother about them at all. But from the beginning of August to the middle of September there is always a chance of a "fall" of these flies on hot sultry afternoons, so during this period it is advisable to have a few dressings of both the red and dark brown varieties in the fly-box.

These are several dressings and I give three as follows:

First, the unusual dressing of the red ant.

HOOK. Nos. 0 to 000 (15-17).

TYING SILK. Orange.

TAG. Bronze peacock herl, three or four turns.

BODY. Orange floss silk.

HACKLE. Red cock's.

WINGS. Light starling, wing feather.

The dressing for the dark brown flying ant is the same as the above, but substituting brown for orange in the silk and floss silk and dark rusty brown for the red hackle.

The second dressing is that of A. Ransome's as given in his book *Rod and Line*.

HOOK. Nos. 0 to 000 (15-17).

TYING SILK. Orange.

BODY. Orange floss, wound on so as to make a pear shaped body.

HACKLE. Red cock's.

WINGS. Two very light grey or light honey dun cock hackle point.

THORAX AND HEAD. Several turns of orange tying silk.

When the fly is oiled, the orange floss silk turns a rich chestnut brown. I used this dressing for a number of years and considered it the best of any, but instead of floss silk for the body, I use Polymer dubbing, chestnut brown for the red ant and very dark brown or black for the dark brown ant, it is, in fact, so dark a brown that it is often called the black ant.

The third dressing I am giving is from a book I recently bought, from a second-hand book shop, called *Design for Angling* with a sub-title *The Dryfly on Western Trout Streams*, it therefore concerns dry-fly fishing in the Western States of America, particularly the north of California and Oregon. It is by

Alexander Macdonald and published by Houghton Mifflin, Boston (Mass.), 1947. In this book, among other dressings, he gives a dressing of the brown ant and a coloured illustration of it. He describes the body as shaped like a miniature hour glass, with a pronounced waist in the centre, between the abdomen and the thorax, and at this waist he made several turns with a red cock's hackle. He made the body and thorax with a rather unusual mixture of peacock herl and dark brown wool. But I prefer using Polymer dubbing for this purpose, as I have done in the previous dressings. I now give a modified dressing as follows:

HOOK. Nos. 0 to 000 (15-17).
SILK. Nylusta, brown, (No. 17 Gossamer).
BODY. Pear shaped with brown Polymer dubbing, or seal fur.
HACKLE. Ginger or light dun cock's.
THORAX. Apple shaped with brown Polymer dubbing.

It will be noted that there are no wings in this dressing but only a hackle at the waist between the body and the thorax. It seems to be a very practical and simple dressing but I have not as yet had the opportunity of giving it a trial.

THE LARGE RED WATER MITE

This mite only seems to inhabit reservoirs and lakes which have a considerable amount of weed growth. If I did not make a practice of taking autopsies of the trout I catch, I would not have realised its importance as an item in the trout's menu. In Talybont reservoir in Breconshire which I fished regularly for some years, several autopsies contained them when the trout were caught near weed beds. In Weir Wood reservoir during the past two seasons (1963 and 1964), I have found them frequently in autopsies and have caught trout on the dressing which I am giving below.

In Helen Mellanby's Book *Animal Life in Fresh Water*, she gives a detailed description and illustration of this mite. The body is globular and red in colour amd grows to 8 mm. in length which is over $\frac{1}{4}$-inch. The legs are black and all except the first pair have swimming hairs, they can therefore swim about with considerable speed and there is little doubt that trout feed on them.

Dressing of the Large Red Water Mite

HOOK. No. 0 to 1 (15-14).
TYING SILK. Nylusta, brown, (No. 17 Gossamer).
BODY. Loaded by winding round the shank several layers of thin copper wire, so as to make the body as bulky as possible. On top of the layers of copper wire, red Polymer or seal's fur dubbing is wound over them to represent the globular body.
HACKLE. Two turns of black hen's or starling's to represent the legs.

THE GEOFFREY BUCKNALL PATTERNS

GEOFF. BUCKNALL is one of the more successful and well-known personalities to have emerged during the upsurge of interest in fly-fishing during the '60's and his prolific pen has produced several best selling books, and articles in the angling press too numerous to mention.

He has never been afraid to dive into controversial "pools", which has always been a stimulating attitude to adopt where angling is concerned, but his main contribution however, has been his ability to pass his knowledge on to others, and there must be many hundreds of adept fly-tyers who owe their dexterity to his expert instruction, to which pleasure must be added his original approach to fly patterns which he also seems to have the knack of passing on.

His two most useful works as far as this book is concerned are *Fly Fishing Tactics on Still Water* published by Frederick Muller Ltd., London, and *Reservoir Trout Fishing* published by Pelham Books. The others are *Fishing Days*, *Big Pike*, and *Fly Fishing Tactics on Rivers*.

These books not only contain improvements on patterns devised by others, but also original concoctions of his own, all based on a sound understanding of fly-fishing in all its aspects.

Although some of the patterns I list here are not his originals, he gave me them to illustrate in the coloured plates, so I consider that this qualifies their inclusion under his name.

DRY FLIES

Hatching Olive Nymph
HOOK. No. 12-14.
TAIL. A slim strip of light olive goose feather.
BODY. As tail, in fact the body can be wound from the buts of the tail strip.
RIB. Fine gold tinsel, oval, or flat, up to thorax only.
THORAX. A "knob" of dark olive seal fur.
WING CASES. A strip of waterhen or any dark wing feather, over thorax only.

HACKLE. A clipped medium or light olive cock hackle.

The coloured illustration will give a good idea of the style one should aim at.

Brown Silver Horns Sedge
HOOK. No. 10-14 up-eye.
BODY. Olive tying silk.
RIB. Fine gold wire.
BODY HACKLE. Darkish brown or furnace, tied "paler" and clipped.

WING. Strip from grouse tail or wing feather (well marked) and tied low over body.

HORNS. Two stripped hackle stalks from a large grizzle hackle. These are realistically marked, and very durable. Note the curved effect.

HACKLE. Darkish brown, wound over wing roots, and clipped. The clipping makes this fly an excellent floater.

Hoolet

HOOK. No. 8-10.

BODY. Bronze peacock herl wound over a strip of cork.

WINGS. Owl or woodcock wing fea-ther tied low over body, either rolled or flat.

HACKLE. Two light red cock hackles wound over wing roots. An excellent dapping or "wake" fly.

Daddy Longlegs

TYING SILK. Brown.

HOOK. 8-10 up eye.

BODY. Brown Floss, Raffia, or Raffine.

LEGS. Knotted pheasant tail fibres, tied in a bunch, sloping backwards, and then divided.

WINGS AND HACKLE. Two gingery hackles wound together, the two points tied in "spent" to form the wings.

WET FLIES

Footballer

HOOK. No. 12-14.

TYING SILK. Grey or dun.

BODY. Black and white horsehair wound from well round bend of hook, to form a slim body of alternate bands of black and white.

THORAX. Mole fur.

HEAD. Peacock herl.

Black Pupa

HOOK. No. 12-14.

BODY. Black horsehair wound from well round bend as "Footballer".

THORAX. Black wool or seal fur.

HEAD. Peacock herl.

Red Pupa

HOOK. No. 12-14.

BODY. Clear horsehair over and underbody of red silk.

THORAX. Red wool or seal fur.

HEAD. Peacock herl.

Green, Yellow, Olive Pupa, etc.

Same tying as for Red Pupa, but using appropriate colour of body silk and thorax material. These coloured dressings of the pupa, including the Red, can be varied by using fluorescent (DFM) silk underbodies, and similar wools for the thorax.

Freshwater Louse

(Variation of the C. F. Walker pattern)

HOOK. No. 14.

LEGS. A grey partridge hackle tied in at bend of hook, wound two or three turns and fixed into the "spent" position with figure-of-eight tyings of silk.

BODY. Pale olive, dun, or any drab or neutral shade of wool or seal fur.

RIB. Finest oval silver tinsel.

Sweeney Todd

HOOK. Long-shanked No. 10-4.

BODY. Black Floss.

RIB. Fine silver oval tinsel.

THROAT. Three or four turns of magenta a fluorescent wool (DFM).

HACKLE. Several fibres from a magenta cock or hens hackle, tied in as a "false" hackle, i.e. underneath only, in the same way as one ties in the wing.

WING. Black squirrel tail fibres, or bucktail in the largest sizes.

Church Fry

Bob Church's variation of the Sweeney Todd.

HOOK. Long-shanked No. 10-4.

BODY. Orange floss silk.

RIB. Flat silver tinsel or Lurex.

THROAT. Magenta (DFM) wool or silk.

HACKLE. A "false" hackle consisting of some fibres from an orange cock hackle.

WING. Grey squirrel tail fibres.

Butcher Tandem

Included here to show how a standard pattern can be converted into a tandem variation.

HOOK. Tandem, No. 12-10.

TAIL. Ibis substitute fibres.

BODY. Flat silver tinsel over both hooks.

RIB. Oval silver tinsel.

HACKLE. Fibres from a black cock's hackle tied as a "false" hackle.

WING. Two strips from the blue feather of a mallard's wing. For larger sizes crow wing feathers can be used.

Other variations on well known patterns by Geoffrey Bucknall—not illustrated.

Green and Brown tube fly

BODY. Alternate turns of green and brown ostrich herl on a one-inch tube, polythene for high level work, metal covered for use in deep water.

RIBBING. Narrow gold Lurex.

HEAD. Peacock herl.

Jersey Herd tube fly

BODY. Gold or copper Lurex on tubes as for Green and Brown tube.

HACKLE. Hot orange goat's hair.

HEAD. Peacock herl.

Peter Ross

TAIL. Tippet fibres.

BODY. Silver Lurex, which is carried on as ribbing over the dubbing.

DUBBING. Red (DFM) wool.

HACKLE. Black hen.

WINGS. Barred teal, grey squirrel tail fibres, or silver baboon.

Blue Damsel Nymph (Dragon Fly)

BODY. Blue Lurex ribbed with black wool on weighted tubes up to 1 inch long.

HACKLE. Dyed blue guinea fowl, or blue bucktail fibres.

HEAD. Peacock herl.

THE RICHARD WALKER PATTERNS

If one observes the dressings and other written material in this section, together with the selection of flies illustrated in the coloured plates, the obvious conclusion is reached that Dick has given a great deal of time and study to producing a series of patterns developed solely for the lake and reservoir fisherman.

I know how long it took him and how much experimentation went into the dressings as I collaborated with him as far as the materials are concerned. I know the painstaking manner in which Dick works, be it on his own ideas or improving on those of other people, just as I know that the ultimate result will be of inestimable value to all us anglers. I think this is because he concentrates his energies on whatever the immediate subject is, and never deviates until he has discovered the best way to do the job being considered. This was most clearly illustrated when he put all his energies into the problem of catching the wily carp, and the fact that his world record breaking specimen ended up in the special tank in the aquarium of the London Zoological Gardens, underlines the point I am trying to make.

Within the pages of this book we have the benefit of the work he has done with regard to the Polystickle, the Muddler Minnow and the shooting-head fly line, and now I hope to lay out the work he has done on natural insects of interest to the lake fisherman. His own interpretations of the Muddler Minnow and Tandem Lures will be found at the end of this chapter, and as I have already stated, they are illustrated in the coloured plates. Clear black and white drawings were supplied by Dick to illustrate his notes on the various patterns, and I only passed them over to Don Downs to supply the finished article so that they would conform to the rest of the black and white illustrations in this book.

THE MIDGE PUPA IMITATIONS
Instructions for making:

Choose tying silk of the right colour for the abdomen. It need not necessarily be "Gossamer" as fine floss or other material can be used. Attach the silk a little way behind the eye of the hook and immediately tie in a bunch of white cock hackle fibres with the points towards the bend of the hook. Wind the tying silk down to about one quarter of the way round the bend of the hook in neat touching turns.

Tie in the ribbing material (white cock hackle stalk or fine silver thread) and, having touched the first set of tying silk (or material used) turns with clear celluloid varnish, wind back again in neat touching turns to where the abdomen will end and the thorax begin. Re-varnish abdomen and, while the varnish is still wet, lay on the ribbing, tie in the end and cut off the waste. At the same point tie in two strands of peacock herl, or feather fibre such as dyed swan,

Fig. 1. Midge Pupa.

turkey, etc., of a suitable colour. (Suggested colours are given later.) Carry silk on to just behind the eye (where the butts of the white cock hackles are projecting) and varnish over these turns of silk. While the varnish is still wet, twist the strands of peacock herl or feather fibre rope-wise and wind on to form the thorax. Tie in and cut-off ends. Finally, lay on two or three turns in front of the butts of the white cock hackles fibres and whip finish. Varnish the whip-finish and cut off the white cock hackle fibres to size. These imitate the

Fig. 2. Hatching or slow-sinking Midge Pupa.

breathing tubes, so should be cut off fairly short. The completed dressing is shown in illustration No. 1.

To slow down the sinking rate and to give the impression of hatching pupa, one can tie in a small bunch of squirrel hair, preferably black, projecting backwards from where the abdomen and thorax meet. This is illustrated in drawing No. 2.

There is no doubt that cock hackle fibres are preferable to floss for imitating breathing tubes on these pupa, and there is reason to think that white cock hackle stalk is better than silver twist or wire for making the abdomen.

The exact nature of the materials is not critical. We usually use "Gossamer" silk for tying small pupa (sizes 14–18) abdomens, with dyed swan thoraces for the Orange and Green pupae, sepia turkey fibres for the Black and Olive ones. For bigger pupae, fine floss silk can be used for the abdomens, and either more feather fibre strands or peacock herl, for the thoraces.

These pupae should be fished very slowly indeed, hardly moving in fact. Or as an alternative, allow to sink approximately two feet then draw steadily two feet, then allow to sink again.

Grease the leader to within two or three inches of the fly for very slow fishing, or to within three feet of the fly for "sink and draw".

THE EPHEMERID NYMPH IMITATIONS

The Sepia Nymph, tied on a No. 12 or 14 hook, has light sepia ostrich herl, dark sepia feather fibre (swan, goose, turkey etc.), and black floss. The tails should be long and the ostrich herl long in the flue. Tying silk should be black.

The Green Nymph can be tied in all sizes from 12 down to 18. For sizes 16 18, dyed swan herl, can replace ostrich, and for sizes 12–14 the ostrich herl should be short in flue. Floss and feather fibre can be any shade from brown-olive to greenish-olive, as the naturals vary tremendously. Tails should be shorter than in the Sepia Nymph.

Both types can be weighted by means of fine copper wire, two layers of touching turns, then built up thicker under the thorax.

Fish these nymphs very slowly at all times. Near surface on a greased leader when trout are showing, otherwise deep on an ungreased leader. In either case *always slow*.

Instructions for making:

At the bend of the hook tie in three or four strands of suitable dyed feather fibre as tails, and at the same point two strands of dyed ostrich herl and one strand of floss, all of suitable colour. Now wind the tying silk back to where the junction of the abdomen and thorax will be, in touching turns, and then varnish these turns with clear celluloid varnish. While this is wet, wind on the ostrich herl with strands twisted rope-wise. Tie down and cut off the waste ends. Wind the floss over the ostrich in open spirals to achieve the effect shown in the illustration tie in but leave waste ends—*do not cut off.*

Tie in a bunch of feather fibres, same as tails, with points projecting over the eye of the hook. Carry silk to behind the eye, wind on the remainder of the floss to form the thorax, tie down and now cut off the waste ends.

Manipulate some of the points of the feather fibres with fingers and silk so that they slope slightly backwards to imitate legs. Bring the rest of the fibres forwards and tie in behind eye to imitate wing cases. Cut off waste and whip-finish and then varnish the head.

Fig. 4. Ephemerid Nymph

CHOMPERS

These are perhaps the easiest of the reservoir flies to tie, and very effective at times.

Instructions for making:

Take a piece of damp Raffine, or a bunch of feather fibres and tie in at the bend of the hook. Also at this point tie in three or four strands of ostrich herl. Colours to use are given at the end of these instructions.

Fig. 5.

Wind the tying silk along the hook-shank in touching turns over the butts of the Raffine or feather fibres, leaving plenty stick out at the back to form the "shell-back" of the fly. Finish winding just behind the eye and cut off any forward-projecting ends which may still protrude. Varnish the windings of tying silk and, twisting the ostrich herl strands into a rope, wind them along to just behind the eye of the hook while the varnish is still wet, tie in and cut off waste ends. (The idea of using the varnish before forming the bodies etc., in the dressings, is for increased durability. John V.)

Bring the Raffine or feather fibres forward, pull taught and tied down behind eye. Cut off waste, from head and whip-finish. Varnish head. (Finished Fly Fig. 5.)

Useful colour combinations for these patterns are:—
Brown Raffine and olive ostrich herl, olive silk.
Clear Raffine and golden-yellow ostrich, black silk.

Brown speckled turkey and golden-yellow ostrich, black silk.
Pale buff Raffine and buff ostrich, brown silk, (Shrimp).
Pea-green Raffine and white ostrich, olive silk.   (Small Corixa).
Brown speckled turkey and white ostrich, olive silk.   (Large Corixa).
Black Raffine or feather fibres, peacock herl instead of ostrich, black silk
(Water Beetle).

These "Chompers" should be fished slowly in small jerks or very slow long
pulls (sink and draw). They can be tied in various sizes—choose the size
appropriate to the natural insect that the colour combination suggests. They can
be very easily weighted by layers of copper wire or lead wound underneath the
dressing.

When using feather fibres instead of Raffine, tie in with the fibre points
forward, then if desired the points can be stroked back to make additional legs.
Fig. 6. For Corixa "Chompers" a tip of silver wound at the bend before the
Raffine or feather fibres are tied in, has improved the taking qualities of this
particular pattern.

Fig. 6.

DRY SEDGES

Despite the opposite views expressed by some reservoir anglers, there are
times when dry sedge imitations can be deadly, and can catch fish when no other
fly would do nearly as well.

All can be dressed on the same principle, as follows, and the dressings are given
after the tying instructions:

On a long-shanked hook, wind the tying silk from behind the eye to the
beginning of the bend. Tie in a wisp of daylight fluorescent floss or wool and
form a tag. Tie in two to five strands of dyed ostrich herl (more for big flies, less
for small ones), and carry the silk in close turns back about two-thirds of the
distance between the tag and eye. Varnish the turns of silk, twist ostrich herl
ropewise, and wind to form the body. Tie in, cut off waste ends and clip the

flue of the body close with sharp scissors. A velvety appearance is achieved by this means.

Tie in a bunch of hackle or feather fibres to lie close to the body and to form the wing. Varnish the roots and cut off the butts of the fibres, and then clip the ends of the fibres flush with the bend of the hook as shown in the illustration.

Tie in, wind on and tie down, two good long stiff cock hackles ahead of wing. Form head with tying silk, whip-finish and varnish.

Do *not* use a spiral body hackle, as is so often advised for Sedges.

Sedge

Some useful Sedge dressings:

Cinnamon Sedge
TYING SILK. Hot orange.
HOOK. No. 10 long-shank.
TAG. Yellow fluorescent floss.
BODY. Buff ostrich herl.
WING. Buff cock hackle fibres, preferably barred.
HACKLES. Ginger or red cock (natural red).

Brown and Green Sedge
HOOK. No. 10 long-shank.
TYING SILK. Hot orange.
BODY. Light green ostrich herl.
WING. Cree (ginger grizzle) cock hackle fibres.
HACKLE. Natural light red cock hackle.

Great Red Sedge
TYING SILK. Orange.
HOOK. No. 8 long-shank.
TAG. Yellow fluorescent floss.
BODY. Mahogany ostrich herl.
WING. Dark natural red cock hackle fibres, preferably barred, or cock pheasant tail fibres.
HACKLES. Natural red cock.

Large Brown Sedge
TYING SILK. Orange.
HOOK. No. 10 long-shank.
TAG. Yellow fluorescent wool or floss.
BODY. Mahogany brown ostrich herl, very fine.
WING. Light brown cock hackle fibres.
HACKLE. Light brown.

H

Grouse Wing
TYING SILK. Black.
HOOK. No. 12 long-shanked.
TAG. White fluorescent floss, very small.
BODY. Dark chocolate ostrich herl or dyed swan herl.
WING. Grouse wing or tail fibres, or dark sepia and brown speckled turkey.
HACKLES. Dark Furnace or dark Coch-y-Bonddu.

Small Buff Sedge
TYING SILK. Primrose.
HOOK. No. 12 long-shank.
TAG. None.
BODY. Pale buff ostrich or swan.
WING. Buff cock hackle fibres.
HACKLES. Buff.

After tying, the sedges should be doped with silicone dressing, and then again immediately before use. A little paraffin-wax dissolved in the dope is a great help with regards to floatability.

Fish these sedges on a fully greased leader, greased right up to the fly. Try letting the fly sit immobile and just giving it an occasional tweak. If that fails skate the fly across the surface very fast so that it sits up on its head hackle ike a speed-boat on its step. This is done by pulling the line with the left hand and simultaneously raising the rod, but don't raise the rod farther than about 60–70 degrees to the horizontal, or there will be no room to strike. After each pull lower the rod about 10 degrees and recover the slack line. Takes may come when the fly is moving, or after it has stopped. This skimming technique can be used at very long range.

Alternatively, try using the sedge on a dropper and either a midge pupa or a yellow "chomper" on the point. If the sedge is drawn under, strike—it acts like a roach float when a trout takes the point fly. But more often the sedge itself is taken.

Choose whichever sedge matches those you see on the water, but the Cinnamon will often catch trout when no naturals are to be seen, especially in August.

Since I prepared this material for the publishers, I have learned that Dick Walker is working on his own book on Reservoir Fly Fishing, and I know from personal experience of his dedication to every detail, that it will be nothing short of a valuable addition to our library shelves.

Dressings of Dick Walker's Lures and Muddlers:

Church Fry Tandem Lure
TYING SILK. Orange.
HOOK. Two in tandem.
BODIES. Fluorescent orange floss or wool.
RIB. Oval silver tinsel.
THROAT HACKLE. Orange.
WING. Grey squirrel tail fibres.
"EYES" Jungle cock—tied in short.

Badger Lure

TYING SILK. Orange.

HOOK. Two in tandem.

BODIES. Fluorescent orange wool.

RIBS. Fine oval silver tinsel.

THROAT. Hot orange cock hackle fibres.

WINGS. Two large badger hackles back to back and as long as the hooks.

"EYES". Two jungle cock feathers tied in short.

Black Muddler Minnow

HOOK. No. 8 long-shank.

TYING SILK. Black.

BODY. Black floss.

RIBS. Fine oval silver tinsel.

WING. Black squirrel tail fibres.

HEAD. Deer body hair made as described on pages 34–37.

HACKLE. None.

Black and White Muddler Minnow

TYING SILK. Scarlet.

HOOK. No. 8 long-shank.

TAIL. None.

BODY. Scarlet floss silk.

RIBS. Fine oval silver tinsel.

WING. Mixed black and white bucktail fibres, or any other hair fibres.

HEAD. Deer body hair made as described on pages 34–37.

HACKLE. None.

Texas Rose Muddler Minnow

TYING SILK. Orange.

HOOK. No. 8 long-shank.

BODY. Orange floss silk.

RIBS. Fine oval silver tinsel.

WING. Yellow bucktail fibres.

HEAD. Deer body hair as described on pages 34–37.

(A feature of the "Muddlers" made by Dick Walker is the length of the head, as shown in the coloured plate. This is about one-third the length of the body.)

Sweeney Todd Tandem

TYING SILK. Black.

HOOKS. Two in tandem.

BODY. Black floss silk.

RIBS. Fine oval silver tinsel.

THROAT. Magenta fluorescent wool.

THROAT HACKLE. Magenta.

WING. Natural Black squirrel tail fibres.

THE DAVID J. COLLYER PATTERNS

I am very happy to include this contribution by David Collyer, as I had the pleasure of watching and assisting his progress from absolute tyro in the field of fly-tying, to a professional position in the same field with a growing reputation for both quality and ingenuity.

It has long been apparent to myself that the finest fly-tyers always come from the ranks of those who have applied themselves meticulously to angling in all its aspects. The concentration, skill, knowledge of the fish's habits, and ability to read the water in which the different types are found, all seem to come to a natural conclusion when their efforts are directed to fly-tying and fly design.

I could classify everyone who has contributed to this book in this category of course, but people like David Collyer and Geoffrey Bucknall who come within professional status must be better known to my readers, together with Richard (Dick) Walker who must be the most well-known all-rounder to emerge during the 50's and 60's.

My experience leads me to typify these three as representatives of the tyers of my generation who have done most to give us the patterns we need for the new waters placed at our disposal, although by so doing I have no intention of detracting from those many others lesser known, or even unknown to the general lake fishing fraternity, who have made a considerable contribution to the wide range of patterns we are now using.

I have included three of David's flies in the coloured illustrations, and although the artist Eric Cumberland-Owen cannot be faulted when it comes to painting the originals, it would not be possible for him to portray the painstaking accuracy that went into these patterns. Every turn of silk was in the right place, so was every feather, and all proportions were meticulously correct.

The script, dressings, and other instructions are as written by David, and I consider that they are sufficient to qualify all I have said in the preceding paragraphs. I like particularly the section devoted to the Matuka, in which he quotes almost word for word, my own opinions with regard to "foreign" flies!

COLLYER'S GREEN, BROWN AND BLACK NYMPHS

Unlike most trout flies, whether used on moving or still waters, these patterns were not brought about by a process of evolution but were the result of one evenings work.

I had long been dissatisfied with the standard types of nymphs quoted in most textbooks on fly-tying, so one afternoon I sallied forth to Weirwood Reservoir at Forest Row in Sussex, armed with a plankton net. I simply searched around until I found a concentration of trout feeding on nymphs then rowed the boat through the middle of them towing the net. The glass jar at its apex was crammed full of a variety of zooplankton including a fair selection of nymphs. I then returned to the fly bench and commenced tying imitations of them. The three resulting patterns have subsequently proved their worth, strangely, not only on lakes but also on rivers from the southern Chalkstreams to the northern becks. They seem to represent to a trout a generalisation of a food-form and are accepted as such.

Collyer's Green Nymph

TAIL. Olive hackle fibres, short, about six to eight strands.

RIB. Oval gold tinsel.

BODY. Dyed olive swan or goose herl.

THORAX. Dyed olive ostrich herl.

METHOD OF DRESSING. Tie in the strands of hackle fibre at the bend of the hook. Tie in the rib at the same point, also the strip of swan or goose. Wind the herl up the body for about two-thirds of it's length and tie in, leave the scrap end attached. Rib the body with the oval gold tinsel, about four turns. Wind the dyed ostrich herl over the remaining third of the body. Tie it as if you were winding the butt on a salmon fly. Carry the scrap end of the swan or goose over and through the ostrich and tie off at the head.

Collyer's Brown Nymph

TAIL. tips of cock pheasant centre tail.

RIB. Oval gold tinsel.

BODY. Cock pheasant centre tail.

THORAX. Dyed brown ostrich herl.

METHOD OF DRESSING. Precisely the same as the green nymph, except one point. The tail consists of the tips of the strands of feather to be used on the body.

Collyer's Black Nymph

TAIL. Black hackle strands.

RIB. Flat, fine silver tinsel.

BODY. Black dyed swan or goose.

THORAX. Black dyed ostrich herl.

METHOD OF DRESSING. As for the previous two patterns, the only difference being in the ribbing material. It has sometimes proved worthwhile to tie in a small piece of white floss silk just behind the head. Hook size. 12 or 14 long-shank.

Mosquito pupae

This fly is a pattern which will prove worth a trial on a bright summers day, preferably in a shady part of the lake. It is simple to dress and should be used just under the surface film on a greased leader. A very gentle twitch of the line every ten seconds or so is all the movement that this fly needs, a twenty yard cast should take at least half-an-hour to recover.

BODY. Stripped peacock herl, taken from the eye feather.

THORAX. Mole or muskrat for dubbing.

METHOD OF DRESSING. Tie in black tying silk at the head and wind down the body in *close* turns, take it well round the bend in the hook. Tie in the stripped peacock herl and wind this almost to the head. Dubb on the fur and wind this just behind the hook eye and tie off. The thorax should be a pronounced round ball.

HOOK SIZE. No. 12.

Grey and Red Matuka

I have yet to see a British trout angler with a Matuka in his fly box, I find this rather surprising as these patterns can be most effective in conditions when no other fly will be accepted. It can be perhaps put down to the fact that these flies require a rather different approach from the normal trout wet-flies in their dressing. As we are so often reminded the British angler is notoriously conservative, an unwillingness to experiment with foreign flies may be the reason for it. In New Zealand all the Matukas have proved their worth, their trout don't differ very much from ours therefore these flies should prove equally effective here. The Grey and Red Matuka is simply a variation of the New Zealand style of dressing that I have found to be most likely to be accepted by British fish. It should be fished either very deep on a sinking line or just under the surface on a floater, the depth of fishing depends on the prevailing conditions.

RIB. Oval silver tinsel.

BODY. Silver grey chenille.

HACKLE. A large bunch of scarlet hackle fibres.

WING. Hen pheasant body feather.

METHOD OF DRESSING. Wind black tying silk down the hook shank almost to the bend and tie in the ribbing tinsel and the chenille. Take close turns of the chenille up the body almost to the head, cut off surplus. Reverse hook in the vice and tie in the beard or false hackle. Turn the hook up the normal way and tie in two hen pheasant body feathers, back to back, after having previously stripped the underside of almost all it's fibres, just leave the fibres at the very tips of the feathers. These make the tail. Lay the feathers vertically along the body and separate the fibres toward the tail, then wind the ribbing tinsel through the wing. Work your way up the body to the head winding the tinsel and at the same time separating the fibres. Tie off at the head. (Pages 149 et seq. illustrate the tying. John V.)

Sinfoil's Fry

I had no hand in the inventing of this fine fry pattern, I was merely instrumental in getting it the publicity that it so richly deserved. The inventor was Mr. Kenneth Sinfoil, head bailiff at Weirwood Reservoir. This is possibly the finest imitation of an extremely young fish fry that is available to the fly fisherman. It should be used when the trout are obviously feeding on the fry of coarse fish, this usually occurs in the shallows when the trout herd them into the trap and then proceed to feed.

UNDER BODY. Flat silver tinsel.
OVER BODY. Polythene strip.
THROAT. Scarlet floss silk.
BACK. The "bad" side of the brown mallard feather.
HEAD. Black tying silk.

METHOD OF DRESSING. Tie in the black silk at the head, don't wind down the body. Tie in the silver tinsel and wind this to about two thirds the length of the body, bring back over itself in even spirals and tie off at the head. Cut off surplus. Take a strip of heavy gauge Polythene and stretch this until it's about a sixteenth of an inch wide, then tie it in at the head, wind it backwards and forwards, up and down the body until a smooth carrot shaped effect is achieved, tie off at the head. Now wind a collar of the scarlet floss silk about an eighth of an inch wide immediately behind the head. A slim strip of the mallard feather is now tied in to lay flat over the back of the fry, this is *not* a wing but merely to give a certain amount of movement to the fly in the water. The head is now built up to a fairly large size, in profile a fry appears to be nearly all head. If it is thought desirable you can now add eyes, these are simply a dab of white varnish and a further dab of black in the centre.

THE JOHN GODDARD* STILLWATER PATTERNS

John Goddard and myself have collaborated on more than one occasion, he with my book *A Further Guide to Fly Dressing*, and me with his fine entomological work *Trout Fly Recognition*. He is also at this moment working on a similar type of book concerned with lake and reservoir life which I know will make a considerable contribution to our knowledge of water activity, both below and above the surface.

I think I can say with little fear of contradiction that John and his close associate Cliff Henry are foremost in the field today as far as the study of the natural diet of trout is concerned. In fact I would not hesitate to class them with Ronalds, Halford, Skues, West or any other famous characters of the past who devoted so much of their time to this branch of our art. Furthermore they have the knowhow and skills to utilise the benefits of modern science to record and preserve the results of their observations, a fact which I can vouch for personally having seen some of the smallest and most delicate specimens of larvae, nymph, adult fly, spinner and spent fly, preserved in plastic blocks literally "without a hair out of place".

Consequently any contribution John may have to make to a collection of fly dressings should be treated with the greatest respect, and it gives me very much pleasure to be in a position to include some of his patterns in this book.

As with most of the individual contributions, his writing is presented verbatim.

"Most of my patterns have been tied to simulate as closely as possible the natural insects and other fauna on which the trout of stillwater from time to time feed. All of these patterns have been proven over a period of time but in some cases the method of fishing is of even more importance than the actual dressing of the fly."

1. The Nevamis Mayfly

Is a pattern developed specifically to overcome the bad hooking properties of many Mayfly patterns. Although originally tied as a river pattern it has proved very effective on some of the large Irish Loughs.

* Author of *Trout Fly Recognition* and *Trout Flies of Stillwater*. published by A. & C. Black and *What Fly is That* by the British Field Sports Society.

Dressing

    HOOK.   Long-shank fine wire No. 8 up-eyed.

    TYING SILK.   Yellow.

    BODY.   Cream seal's fur wound thickly—body hackle-large honey cock tied in at tail and wound to shoulder and then clipped to $\frac{1}{4}$-inch of body at shoulder, sloping to $\frac{1}{8}$-inch at tail.

    RIB.   Oval gold tinsel.

    WINGS.   V-shaped hackle fibre wings using a large pale blue dun cock.

    HACKLE.   Small furnace cock ($\frac{1}{2}$-inch fibres).

    TAIL.   Three long pheasant tail fibres.

2. The Hatching Mayfly

This pattern has proved very effective and is also an excellent hooker. It is tied to represent the adult insect emerging from its nymphal case in the surface film, and is finished with the tail section of the artificial submerged.

Dressing

    HOOK.   Long-shank fine wire No. 8.

    TYING SILK.   Yellow.

    BODY.   Tail half—cock pheasant tail fibres. Head half—cream seal's fur.

    RIB.   Gold wire or narrow gold lurex.

    WINGS.   V-shaped hackle fibre wings using a large pale blue dun cock.

    HACKLE.   Small furnace cock tied thickly.

    TAIL.   Tips of three pheasant tail fibres.

3. The Last Hope

An exceptionally killing pattern originally developed to represent the Pale Watery dun or any small pale coloured river insects. It has now proved to be equally effective to represent the Angler's Curse (Caenis) of stillwater. A very simple pattern to tie but it is essential to use a very short-fibred hackle. Although essentially a dry-fly, it is also extremely effective fished slowly as a wet fly in the surface film, to represent a hatching caenis nymph.

Dressing

    HOOK.   17 or 18 up-eyed fine wire.

    TYING SILK.   Pale yellow.

    BODY.   Two or three Norwegian goose or condor herls grey buff.

    HACKLE.   Dark honey very short in flue.

    TAIL.   Honey dun cock, six to eight fibres.

4. The Shrimper

This is a tying to imitate the freshwater shrimp. It is tied as a weighted pattern to sink quickly and should be fished on a floating or sinking tip-line in the shallow margins in the vicinity of weed. It should be retrieved slowly along the bottom with frequent pauses.

Dressing

HOOK. No. 10 to 14 down-eyed Limerick.

TYING SILK. Orange.

BODY. Copper wire wound from eye to bend, thickening in centre to form hump. Tie in strip of natural P.V.C. about $\frac{1}{8}$ inch wide at bend followed by olive marabou silk and a honey coloured hackle. Wind olive marabou to eye followed by hackle palmer fashion, and then stretch strip of P.V.C. over the top of the body and hackles and tie in at eye. Finally trim excess hackles from along side of body.

N.B. To represent mating colour of shrimp during June, July tie in orange fluorescent silk sparsely on top of marabou.

5. Red or Green Larvae

A simple dressing to simulate the larvae of some of the larger Chironomids. The larvae of these flies are found in large numbers in or on the silt or mud. When they move it is with a figure of eight lashing movement which is quite impossible to imitate, but as they are often observed lying almost still on the bottom the most effective method of fishing this pattern, if one has patience, is as follows. It must be fished from the bank or anchored boat. Cast into medium or deep water using a sinking line preferably. Allow the artificial to lay on the bottom for a long period occasionally giving the line a slight twitch (ideal for fishing during the lunch break).

Dressing

HOOK. Long-shank down-eyed No. 8 to 12.

TYING SILK. Brown.

TAIL. A piece from the curly section of an Ibis quill (red). This should be approximately $\frac{1}{2}$-inch long, and must be a piece from a curled feather, otherwise the right action cannot be imparted when the fly is fished. The stop-start motion will cause the curled part of the tail to straighten out and recurl, providing a certain amount of animation. As an alternative, a curved tip of a red or green cock hackle may be used.

BODY. Crimson or olive condor herl covered with fluorescent floss of same colour.

RIB.   Narrow silver lurex.

THORAX.   Several turns of buff condor herl.

6. The Hatching Midge Pupa

As this pattern has to be fished either without movement or exceedingly slowly, it is important that the artificial pupa resembles the natural as closely as possible.   The method of fishing is equally important and is as follows.   A floating line is used with the cast lightly greased.   A large well-greased dry sedge pattern is fished on the point, with two or three pupae tied directly on to the cast at twelve-inch intervals; the nearest should be at least a yard away from the dry sedge on the point.   This pattern should be tied on a straight eyed hook and either tied directly into the cast or held in position on the cast by blood knots.   This pattern and method have proved most effective during calm conditions, during a widespread rise to the pupa (buzzer) when trout are often most difficult to catch.   The artificial pupae may be cast in the path of a rising fish without movement or may be cast at random and retrieved with occasional very slow pulls.   The colour and size of pupae used should be dictated by the colour and size of the natural pupae hatching at the time.   An effective alternative method of fishing this artificial when the trout are not feeding on the surface is to use a weighted nymph on the point and one or two artificial pupae on droppers.   Fish sink and draw with a floating or sinktip line in water of medium depth but retrieve as slowly as possible.

Dressing

HOOK.   Straight-eye round bend No. 10–14.

SILK.   As body colour.

BODY.   Black, brown, orange, red or green maribou silk, rib with silver lurex and then cover with opaque P.V.C.

TAG.   White hen hackle fibres projecting about $\frac{1}{8}$ inch from tail tied in well round bend of hook.

THORAX.   Green peacock or buff Condor herl.

HEAD FILAMENTS.   Loop or bunch of white hen hackle fibres tied through thorax but facing upward and forward over eye of hook.

N.B.   With the red pattern I often tie in a hot orange pad on top of thorax to represent the distinctly orange wing cases of this particular pupa.

7. The Small Hatching Midge

At certain times during the summer on most waters occur quite large hatches of some of the smaller midges, usually of a brown, red or green coloration. When these small pupae are hatching, usually during the hours of daylight, the trout often become pre-occupied feeding on them and are very difficult to catch. With this pattern I have achieved a certain amount of success but it must be fished only partly submerged in the surface film, as it is meant to represent the adult midge transposing from the pupal case. When trout are feeding on these emerging midges the rise form is unmistakable as they usually rise repeatedly in a circular pattern barely breaking the surface with their neb as they sip them down. This pattern should be fished with little or no movement on the point, or on the point and top dropper from a boat.

Dressing

HOOK. Down-eyed No. 16.

TYING SILK. Brown.

BODY. Two turns of silver lurex round bend of hook followed by main body of dark red, green or brown condor herl.

RIB. Narrow silver lurex.

THORAX. Buff condor herl.

HACKLE. Small honey cock hackle tied in immediately behind eye.

8. P.V.C. Nymph

Initially developed as a river pattern to represent any of the Olive nymphs it has proved an exceptionally killing pattern, and has since proved to be equally effective on stillwater where Lake and Pond Olive nymphs are found. Fish in the vicinity of weed in shallower water to represent the Pond Olive nymph or deeper water for the Lake Olive. Most effective method sink and draw as slowly as it is possible to retrieve.

Dressing

HOOK. Down-eyed No. 12 or 14.

TYING SILK. Yellow.

BODY. Cover shank of hook with fine copper wire, forming hump near eye to represent thorax. Tie in silk at bend then body materials; first of all three strands of olive condor herl leaving the fine tips protruding to represent tails. Follow with narrow silver lurex, and then a one-sixteenth inch wide strip of olive dyed P.V.C. Take herl up to eye and tie in, wind silk back over hump to rear of thorax, bring lurex rib up and tie in followed by P.V.C. to cover body to this point, then continue back to eye with silk and tie in three blackish pheasant tail fibres doubled and redoubled over top of thorax.

9. The Phantom Fly

A dry fly tied to represent the female as she alights on the water to oviposit her eggs, this is usually in the margins of lakes in the late evening.

HOOK. Up-eyed No. 14.
TYING SILK. Orange.
BODY. Grey condor herl with a wide rib of olive dyed P.V.C.
HACKLE. Honey cock, tied in well back from eye.
WINGS. White hackle points tied spent.

10. The Phantom Pupa

This species is very prolific on many waters. The artificial should be fished on its own on the point, and retrieved in small jerks a little off the bottom.

Dressing

HOOK. Down-eyed No. 16.
TYING SILK. Brown.
BODY. One strand of white marabou silk with a narrow silver lurex rib.
THORAX. Formed from two strands of orange marabou silk.
    Finally the whole body and thorax is covered with clear P.V.C.

11. The Pond Olive Spinner

Often referred to as the Apricot spinner due to its very distinctive colouring, it is one spinner that does really call for a special artificial to specifically represent it. Should be fished in, not on, surface film.

Dressing

HOOK. Up-eyed 12 or 14.
TYING SILK. Orange.
BODY. Apricot coloured condor herl covered with olive pale dyed P.V.C.
WINGS. Pale blue hackle tips tied spent.
HACKLE. Dark honey cock. A bunch of these fibres tied in under each
    spent wing in place of the traditional type of hackle.
TAILS. Fibres from a pale badger hackle.

12. Ant—Black or Brown

Although this pattern may not be used very often, it is extremely effective on those somewhat rare occasions when a fall of ants occur. It is fished as a dry-fly but with occasional animation.

Dressing

HOOK. Up-eyed No. 14.
TYING SILK. Black, brown or orange according to colour of natural ant on
    water.
BODY. Two small cylindrical pieces of cork split and bound round shank

of hook, one near bend the other near eye. Cover with above choice of tying silk from bend to eye and varnish.

WINGS. Two white hackle tips tied spent but at an angle towards rear.

HACKLE. Black or Rhode Island red cock hackle to match tying silk used.

13. The Snail

During most seasons there occurs on many stillwaters a mass migration of snails to the surface where they float in the surface film, for hours or sometimes even days. When this takes place the trout will nearly always become pre-occupied feeding on them to the exclusion of all other forms of food and only a pattern to represent these snails will succeed. This artificial was originally developed by the well-known amateur fly dresser, Cliff Henry, and over the years has accounted for very many trout.

Dressing

HOOK. No. 10 to 14 Down-eyed wide gape.

TYING SILK. Black.

BODY. A flat-topped pear-shaped section of cork is formed partly split and bound lightly over shank of hook with flat section facing eye. This is then covered with stripped peacock quill except for last two turns near flattened top representing pad of snail for which bronzed peacock herl should be used.

14. The Adult Midge

A dressing to represent the newly hatched adult winged midge as it rests on the surface after hatching. This pattern should be fished as a dry-fly with little or no movement when the adults are on the water, and the trout appear to be taking them as they occasionally do. It should be tied in several colours and sizes to match the adult that happens to be hatching at the time.

Dressing

HOOK. Up-eyed No. 10 to 14.

TYING SILK. Brown.

BODY. Marabou silk in red, brown or green wound thickly to give body a cylindrical appearance. This is ribbed with silver lurex and covered with opaque P.V.C.

HACKLE. Dark honey cock.

WINGS. Pale blue cock hackle tips tied in spent fashion but at an angle towards tail.

15. Sedge Pupa

A very killing pattern from July onwards. It is intended to represent the pupae of various Sedge-flies, as they ascend to the surface in the first stages of transformation to the winged fly. It should be fished fairly slowly in medium to shallow water. The artificial is dressed in either orange or green, two of the most common colours of the natural.

Dressing

HOOK. Long-shank wide gape No. 10 or 12.

TYING SILK. Brown.

BODY. Cream, orange *or* olive green seal's fur. The latter two colours may be covered lightly with fluorescent floss of same colour and all are ribbed with narrow silver lurex.

THORAX. Dark brown condor herl.

WING CASES. Pale brown condor herl. Four to six strands are tied in with body materials at bend of hook. These are brought over the top of body and tied in at head, and then doubled and redoubled to form the wing pads.

HACKLE. Honey hen hackle tied sparsely 1½–2 turns.

THE "TAFFY" PRICE PATTERNS

I have known "Taffy" Price for a long time now, and watched his development from a keen and enthusiastic beginner to the ranks of those semi-professional tyers that have "blossomed" in this country during the last ten years or so.

Like Geoffrey Bucknall, Dave Collyer, and others who have contributed to this book, he has not been content to follow slavishly the recommended dressings of others, and the results of his experiments I am very pleased to include here. He may not be quite as well known as some of my other collaborators, so the few notes I have appended concerning him may be of some interest, and were culled from the many conversations I have had with him, during the many years we have done business together. The notes following each fly are, of course, his own.

He has lived in the South East of England for the last seventeen years, having moved down from North Wales, and it was not long before he was given the nickname "Taff", a name by which all his friends and acquaintances know him.

He has always been interested in all branches of angling, but his greatest interest lies with fly-fishing in all its facets, although he does enjoy his monthly visits to Deal sea fishing as a change from waving the fly rod about.

He has avoided putting his theories etc., to print as he feels there are enough experts far better qualified than himself to cause controversy each month in the Angling Press. As he says "If I could fish as well as I theorise, I would be an angling expert *par exellence*, but I cannot, so I remain quite happy with more than one blank day.

"I would like to tie flies as a full time occupation, but the retail price of flies being what it is and the amount of salary I get at my present occupation deters me, so I stick to my semi-professional-cum-amateur status and get the best of both worlds."

His fishing is confined to a local lake and most of the South Eastern reservoirs with occasional sorties to Grafham, North Wales, and Devon.

His fly-tying activities are confined now to tying solely for K. Summers & Son of Orpington, as this allows him some time for fishing, for in the past he found himself busy at the vice tying flies for three shops and numerous individuals, whilst everyone else was out fishing!

He started tying flies for two reasons. One, he could not purchase, locally, flies that he wanted; secondly, he found when fishing the Welsh mountain streams he left more flies and broken casts in the trees than he caught fish. Within two years he had become reasonably proficient and was able to fill a local demand for flies. From the shop in Orpington he has supplied flies for fishing in South Africa, Portugal, Denmark, Norway, and both coasts of America, as well as for most parts of the four home countries and Eire.

Whilst the bulk of his time is taken by tying the usual standard patterns, he endeavours to devote time to the creation of patterns of his own design, or at least flies that he can find no reference to in the many books he possesses. Over the last two seasons he has experimented with the Streamer and Bucktail type of fly. The following list of dressings are of the conventional and of the streamer variety.

Chris's Orange Sedge (Dry)

This pattern is the invention of Chris Padley of Tunbridge Wells, a well-known angler at Weirwood, and treasurer of the Weirwood Fly Fishing Association. He originally tied this pattern with a hot orange hackle in lieu of a furnace hackle. The following day at Weirwood he rose and caught four trout in succesion, all of about 1½lbs. which for Weirwood are not bad fish. It has caught many fish since, in fact the trout caught on this pattern must run into many hundreds, why they take it so avidly I don't know, but they do.

BODY. Hare's ear dubbing.
RIB. Flat gold lurex.
WING. Patrridge Wing, rolled and tied flat across the back.
HACKLE. Hot orange in front of wing.
HOOK SIZE. No. 12 or 14 up-eyed.

Black Gnat (Dry)

This second fly is just a variation of the conventional Black Gnat, the only difference to the normal dressing is in the material used for the wings. For the wing I use the small feathers from base of the Jungle Cock cape which are too small to use for any other purpose, i.e. cheeks etc.

TAIL. Black cock hackle fibres.
BODY. Black tying silk.
HACKLE. Black cock.
WING. The small tufty feathers from the base of Jungle Cock neck tied upright or spent.
HOOK. Up-eyed No. 14-16.

Black Butcher (Wet)

This fly was put on in desperation one hot day in August at Grafham. The reservoir was flat, calm and no fish rising. I fished this fly slowly along the dam wall and it took for me a brown trout over three pounds, the largest fish caught that day. An autopsy on the trout revealed it had been feeding exclusively on snail. It may well be that the trout took this fly for a snail, the fly's shape is snail-like in silhouette, but who knows what a trout thinks?

TAIL. Black cock fairly long and on the same plane as hook shank.
TAG. Flat silver.
BODY. Tapered black floss.
RIB. Flat silver rib.
HACKLE. Black cock tied as a false hackle.
WING. Black crow, wide slips tied horizontally right to the bend of the hook.

For the last two seasons I have fished streamer pattern flies. I felt that a lot more work with this kind of fly was needed. Basically streamers and buck tails can be divided into two distinct groups, one, the lure designed as a direct imitation of a bait fish, i.e. a minnow, a stickleback, or fry of many species. The other class are the more bizarre highly-coloured creations that tempt trout to take out of anger, curiosity, or out of sheer amusement.

The first four dressings are for lures of the small fish imitation category, the rest are of the more exotic variety. All the patterns listed have caught for me and my friends more trout this season than any other flies in the past. These flies are not hurled far out into the reservoir or lake and then stripped in as fast as possible, as some small fry purists suggest; they can or should be fished with all the finesse of nymph fishing.

Minnow Streamer

This fly is fished when the trout are obviously taking the species, it should be fished with slow pulls, with occasional pauses and faster spurts now and again. In fact all Streamers and Bucktails should be fished with movement as near to a natural fish as possible, not as a jet-propelled aquatic rocket; fished fast, some-times—yes, but alternate with common sense.

TAIL. Blue Dun hackle fibres.
RIB. Silver lurex.
BODY. White floss tapered fish-like.
HACKLE. Scarlet cock false hackle for the male minnow, Blue dun for female.

WING. Two cock hackles dark olive; either side, strips of black and white barred teal.

CHEEK. Jungle cock very short.

HEAD. Olive green white underneath.

HOOK. Longshank No. 8.

Hairy Minnow

Not only has this bucktail taken Rainbows and Brown trout, it took a Roach of over 1½ lbs. on what would have been a blank day.

TAIL. Small tuft of DFM Red wool (fluorescent).

BODY. Flat silver.

RIB. Oval silver.

WING. Dark green bucktail, white bucktail underneath.

UNDER WING OR HACKLE. Reverse hook in the vice, tie in white bucktail to bend of hook then a small tuft of red bucktail at the throat.

HEAD. Black, with white painted eye, black pupil.

HOOK. Long-shanked No. 8–10.

Brown Trout Streamer

Whilst fishing the outflow of our lake for a large brown trout that lay under some trees, I had a thumping take, a trout I thought until I netted a Jack Pike of just under 3lbs. I believe a lot more work is to be done in the field of streamer flies for Pike in this country as they are fished most successfully in the U.S.A.

TAIL. A tuft of olive green hackle.

BODY. Thin tapered green floss.

RIB. Flat gold tinsel or lurex.

WING. Six cock hackles; two fiery brown hackles back to back, two dark olive hackles either side, followed by two badger hackles.

HACKLE. Dark green olive tied false with a few strands of long white hackle fibres the length of the body tied under the dark olive.

CHEEK. Jungle cock a quarter the length of wing.

HOOK. Long-shank No. 4, 6 and 8.

Pink Rainbow Streamer

Fished on a single long-shanked hook this fly is very effective, but where very large trout lurk that are in the habit of taking plump stockfish a tandem fly is the better bet, tied on two long-shanked hooks.

TAIL. Olive green hackle fibres.

BODY. White wool.

RIB. Silver oval.

WING. Four pale pink hackles extending just beyond the hook, green peacock herl over, or two dark olive cock hackles.

UNDER WING. Two narrow white cock hackles pointing downwards to cover the bite of the hook.

HACKLE. Short tuft of olive hackle at the throat and in between the white.

CHEEK. Jungle cock tied short.

HEAD. Black.

HOOK. Long-shank No. 4, 6 and 8 or two long-shanks in tandem giving a fly four to five inches long.

Now for the second category of fly, the lurid tempter! One of my favourite colours has always been Orange. The following three patterns are variations of the same theme, the colour orange. All three patterns have taken their fair share of trout.

Orange Streamer

TAIL. None.

BODY. Orange floss.

RIB. Gold tinsel or lurex.

HACKLE. None.

WING. Two hot orange hackles back to back, two Badger hackles either side of them.

CHEEK. Jungle cock a quarter the length of wing.

HOOK. Long-shanked No. 6, 8, 10.

Orange Bucktail

TAIL. None.

BODY. Oval gold tinsel size 8.

WING. Orange bucktail not too heavily dressed.

HACKLE. None.

HEAD. Black with white painted eye and black pupil.

HOOK. Long-shanked No. 8–10.

Orange Muddler

This fly is a variation of the now popular muddler minnow. Fished just under the surface so that it left a wake when retrieved in a medium fast recovery, it accounted for me, three rainbows in succession, then for my friend it took a further five, best of which weighed two pounds. The rainbows could be seen following the fly in, before the take.

TAIL. Orange hackle fibres.

BODY. Flat silver or gold lurex.

WING. Orange bucktail.

HEAD. Clipped deer hair as for conventional muddler.

Banded Squirrel Bucktail

TAIL. White squirrel tail with black band, tie in at the black portion.

BODY. Pale Mauve wool or white wool, fairly bulky.

RIB. Flat silver narrow.

WING. Barred squirrel (white tip, black bar, brown root).

HACKLE. White bucktail length of body, red bucktail tied short at throat.

I seem to have taken only brown trout on this fly especially when there was a lot of colour in the water.

Painted Lady Streamer

Using some feathers I had left on the fly-tying table after tying some salmon flies, I created, for want of a better word, the following fly, and for want of a better name I called it the Painted Lady. Fished at dusk or when nearly dark it has taken both rainbows and browns.

TAIL. A bunch of dyed blue guinea fowl body feather (spotted fibres).

BODY. Tapered black floss thin.

RIB. Flat silver tinsel or lurex.

WING. Four black cock hackles.

CHEEK. Jungle cock a quarter wing length.

HACKLE. Magenta.

HEAD. Black.

HOOK. Long-shanked No. 4, 6, 8.

Black and Orange Marabou

Marabou flies are extremely popular in the U.S.A. for most species of game fish. This is due in the main to the excellent mobility of the feather in the water, which the fish find irresistible. Fished deep, early in the season when the water is cold, and the fish hungry, it can be a killer.

TAIL. Orange or red D.F.M. wool.

BODY. Oval or flat silver.

WING. Black Marabou feathers, strip the fibres and tie them in small bunches.

CHEEK. Jungle cock not too long.

HACKLE. Hot orange cock.

HOOK. Three-quarter Long-shanked No. 8–10.

THE ROY MASTERS PATTERNS

FLIES FOR CHEW, BLAGDON AND OTHER WATERS OF THE BRISTOL WATERWORKS UNDERTAKINGS

Roy is my wife's nephew, but I have no hesitation in saying that his efforts are not included in this book for this reason. I taught him both to fly fish and tie flies, and he rewarded my efforts by taking a 5 lb. 2 oz brown trout from Chew Valley lake at the end of his first "solo" year. As I have not included a fish of these proportions in any of my catches so far, I feel sure that nobody will accuse me of nepotism.

As with my other collaborators, his script and dressings are verbatim, the only personal observation on my part being to point out that his dressing of the "Chief" shows how he has taken a well-established pattern "Chief Needabeh" and converted it to his own requirements.

The Chief
HOOK.   No. 8–10 long-shanked hook.
TAG.   Silver tinsel.
BODY.   Firebrand fluorescent floss silk, scarlet.
RIB.   Oval silver tinsel.
WINGS.   Two yellow hackles back to back inside, with two scarlet hackles outside with a jungle cock eye each side.   (See note at bottom).
HACKLE.   Mixed scarlet and yellow cock.
HEAD.   Black varnish.

The yellow inside hackles of the wing may be hen hackles, but the outside scarlet hackles must be cock hackles.

The cock hackles also must be a bright scarlet and of the slim pointed type; this gives a striking contrast to the fly.

The Cree Streamer
HOOK.   No. 8 long-shanked.
TAIL.   A thick bunch of light brown hen hackle fibres.
BODY.   First wind lead wire along hook shank, then coat with varnish and wind in silver lurex from ready cut reel or cut from a strip.   Allow to dry.

WINGS. Cock hackles from the Cree (coloured grizzle) cape. Take four hackles; two small, about the length of the silver body, and two large. The large hackles when tied in should just extend past the tail.

Put the small hackles back to back inside the large hackles and tie in, then tie in jungle cock eyes.

HACKLE. Mixed yellow and scarlet cock swept back over wing when tied in.

HEAD. Black varnish.

DRY FLIES

The Cree Sedge

HOOK. No. 13 wide-gape or smaller.

TYING SILK. White.

BODY. Cree hackle, or hackles, wound along hook shank and trimmed down very short to a cigar shape.

WINGS. A bunch of natural red cock hackles, tied in to lie along body and trimmed at end in a sort of fan shape.

HACKLE. Cree hackle of correct size from a Cree cape.

Curse Spinner

HOOK. No. 18 wide-gape up-eyed.

TAIL. Three white cock hackle fibres.

BODY. White seal's fur or condor herl.

HACKLE. Very small white cock, trimmed flat at underside.

TYING SILK. The best type of tying silk to use for such a small fly is a thread called Nylusta, or the type of fine thread used for repairing nylon stockings.

NYMPHS

Curse Nymph

HOOK. No. 16.

RIB. Fine oval silver tinsel. (See note)

BODY. White seal's fur.

TYING SILK. Stocking thread.

When winding rib make the turns very close together so that seal's fur fibres are bound down tight and will stand out.

Fluorescent Green Nymph

HOOK. Nos. 10, 11, 12 and 13.

BODY. First under body. Lime fluorescent floss silk. Cover with light green monofilament. (See instructions)

HACKLE. Brown partridge.

HEAD. Peacock herl.

Instructions for tying body of Green Nymph

When tying the body of Green Nymph, make the under body cigar shape. Under body must be fluorescent lime and wound on very tight. The monofilament must also be wound on very tightly over the floss silk, each turn neatly next to the other until the lime fluorescent floss is completely covered. This will give a very good translucent body.

The monofilament should be about 12 lb. B.S. and of a bright light green; some sea-fishing monofilaments sold are often this colour and one spool will last a long time.

When tying in monofilament the end which you intend to tie in may be flattened. This will make it easy to tie on to hook shank.

As you may know, the Green Nymph is one of Mr. T. C. Ivens' Nymphs originally, but the fluorescent Green Nymph is a fly I have based on Mr. Ivens' fly, but the use of fluorescent material gives a better translucent effect to the body.

R. M.

METHOD OF FISHING

THE CHIEF AND CREE STREAMER

These two flies being Streamer flies can be fished exactly the same way. Both flies fish well deep with a wet line and can be fished fast or in short jerks. A good method is to fish these flies across the path of fish which are sticklebacking. The fly must be stripped in fast and the "Cree" Streamer gives best results fished in this way. My last two fish, both Brownies, were caught on the Cree in this way at Blagdon. Both took the fly head on and were hooked deep in the scissors; one 2 lb. and the other 2 lb. 2 oz.

The "Chief" can give good results fished this way but does, I think, better fished deep down near the bottom of the lake. When fished deep the "Chief" can be fished in by yard-long pulls with a pause in between. This can give a hot afternoon a good result. Another method is to cast the "Chief" to those fish which rise to a minute fly on the surface, which you cannot imitate, and fish the fly as soon as it hits the surface. The "Chief" will then leave a wake behind it and if a fish follows the fly another wake will appear behind the fly. The take should be a boil on the surface and some fish fail to connect first time. If this happens, do not stop fishing the fly as some fish will take the fly again a few yards further in.

CURSE SPINNER AND NYMPH

Fish both these flies when fish are feeding on caenis or angler's curse, the Spinner being cast out and left in the surface film or cast in front of rising fish. The nymph must hang just under the surface film and, given the odd twitch or cast in front of rising fish, will give a good result.

CREE SEDGE (DRY FLY)

Fished exactly the same way as any other lake sedge fly. Good results when cast in front of rising fish in the evening, or just cast out and left on surface. Give the odd twitch to fly as an attraction.

FLUORESCENT GREEN NYMPH

Can be fished along the bottom or just under surface. Move very slowly under surface and continuous hand wind along the bottom.

FARLOW'S "MURDERERS"

This series of flies was brought to my notice by Richard Aylot, a member of the famous fishing tackle firm of C. Farlow & Co. Ltd., and also a very keen lake fly fisherman. They have accounted for some very big fish at Grafham, particularly in the early part of the season, and although they appear at first sight to be standard streamer-fly types, the addition of the D.F.M. (fluorescent) materials is a distinctive feature.

The hooks to use are long-shanked in sizes 4 to 8, and the wings should be dressed well beyond the bend of the hook.

No. 1 Black

TAG. Red (DFM) floss, two or three turns.
BODY. Black floss.
RIB. White (DFM) floss.
WINGS. Two black cock hackles, back to back.
HACKLE. Black.
HEAD. Black varnish.

No. 2 Gold

TAG. Red (DFM) floss.
BODY. Embossed gold tinsel. (I think Mylar tubing would do on this pattern and No. 3—J.V.).
HACKLE. Dyed red cock hackle.
WINGS. Two grizzle cock hackles back to back.
"EYES". Two small jungle cock feathers tied close to head.
HEAD. Black varnish.

No. 3 Silver

TAG. Lime (DFM) floss.
BODY. Embossed silver tinsel.
HACKLE. Cock hackle dyed fluorescent yellow.
WINGS. Two grizzle cock hackles back to back.
"EYES". Two jungle cock feathers tied close to head.
HEAD. Black varnish.

WELSH PATTERNS

A selection of Welsh patterns which he recommends, for the Llanberis lakes in particular, and for other lakes of North Wales, by Mr. G. O. Jones, 1957 captain of the Welsh International Fly Fishing Team:

Ceiliog Hwyaden a Chorff Gwin
TAIL. Fibres from brown mallard flank.
BODY.   Claret seal's fur.
RIB.   Gold wire.
WINGS.   Brown mallard.
HACKLE.   Black or claret.

Brech yr Iar (Alder)
BODY.   Peacock herl dyed magenta.
WINGS.   Speckled hen wing quill.
HACKLE.   Black.

Starling Corff Du
TAIL.   Blue dun hackle fibres.
BODY.   Black silk.
RIB.   Flat silver.
HACKLE.   Blue dun.
WING. Starling wing quill. ("Blae and Black" (?)).

Petrisen Corff Paun
BODY.   Bronze peacock herl.
HACKLE.   Brown partridge back.

Petrisen Corff Twrch
TAIL.   Brown partridge back fibres.

BODY.   Mole fur.
RIB.   Silver.
HACKLE.   Brown partridge back.

Ceiliog Hwyaden Corff Piws
BODY.   Purple seal's fur.
RIB.   Gold.
WINGS.   Bronze mallard.
HACKLE.   Black or purple.

Petrisen Corff Blewyn Ysgyfarnog
BODY.   From hare's ear.
RIB.   Silver.
HACKLE.   Brown partridge.

Ceiliog Hwyaden a Chorff Melyn Budr
BODY.   Yellow seal fur.
RIB.   Gold or silver.
WINGS.   Bronze mallard.
HACKLE.   Ginger or yellow.

Cyffl ogyn Corff Gwyrdd
BODY.   Green seal's fur.
RIB.   Silver.
WINGS.   Woodcock wing quill.
HACKLE.   Ginger or green.

DEREK MOSELEY'S IRISH MAYFLIES (FOR LAKES)

The advent of the mayfly hatch on the Irish Loughs is anticipated as eagerly each year as the hatch in England. One great difference, however, is that whereas the artificial fly has long been the recognised lure for the English streams, it has been customary to use the natural fly on the Loughs.

I personally have had no experience in Ireland, but Mr. Moseley, late of West Wickham, Kent (and now resident in Ireland), who has fished year after year in those waters, has evolved three flies which kill fish on the Loughs, even when the natural is being refused.

He has very kindly passed on the dressing of these flies, together with the method of tying and the way to fish them.

Green Mayfly (Sub-imago): "Ginger"

This pattern has been used on all ordinary occasions when the greenfly is hatching, with definite success since 1939. It is appreciated that, to the human eye at any rate, this fly does not resemble a mayfly, but the fact remains that it is taken, apparently with relish, by trout during a greenfly hatch when other patterns are refused.

HOOK. No. 9 or 10 long-shanked.

TYING SILK. Olive.

WHISKS. Three cock pheasant tail fibres tied in cocked up at 45 degrees and varnished, and separated (1 inch).

BODY. Natural cream or white raffia, with gold rib.

BODY HACKLE. Deep golden dun cock.

WING HACKLE. One each, dyed deep golden dun cock and natural deep red cock.

Tie in body and body hackle as for "Female Spinner" (see p. 141).

Prepare one of each type of the wing hackles, *including* some of the lower part where they go soft and dull. Lay the two hackles together with the red on top and tie in at eye. Wind tying silk back to body so that hackles are wound over it. Wind the two hackles together till the body is reached. Carry tying silk back through hackles and build up head and finish off. Varnish head. Part and trim the hackles underneath as for "Female Spinner", i.e. 90 degrees.

Notes.—In all the patterns the wing hackles will go on better if a layer of tying silk is wound on first. All hackle points not needed are, of course, cut off, after fastening down. The two hackles on the Green Mayfly will mix themselves as they are wound on, but it is better to make the golden hackle wider than the red.

Female Spinner (Imago): "Jimmy R"

Used with consistent results since 1935. Used when there is a genuine "fall" of spinner in the evenings, when the females blow or fly out from the bushes on their last journey, and are fully fertilised. This fly will float in quite a "chop" —often a necessity, as the flies sometimes go out quite a distance and do not always choose a flat calm to do it.

> HOOK. No. 9 or 10 long-shanked.
> WHISKS. Three cock pheasant tail fibres, tied in flat and varnished ($1\frac{1}{2}$ inch).
> BODY. Natural cream or white raffia, with gold rib.
> BODY HACKLE. White cock.
> WING HACKLE. Rusty black cock hackle or dark iron blue cock hackle.

The body should be varnished with clear Cellire before winding the body hackle. Leave a good eighth inch between body and hook eye. The wing hackle is tied in at the eye and wound to the body. Finish off tying silk at eye; form a good "head", which should be well varnished. The hackle is then trimmed *underneath* the hook-shank to form a parting of 90 degrees. The top half of the hackle is left untrimmed.

Male (Cock) Mayfly Spinner (Sub-imago): "Purple Tail"

This pattern has been used from 1948 onwards, and will also kill when a "fall" is taking place. Its main use, however, comes when on hot days or in sheltered corners during the day, the cock imago flies down to drink and gets trapped in the scum, generally well into the mayfly season. These flies get gathered in patches and when a fish finds them he will eat the lot, but will *not*, as a rule, look at any normal artificial. This fly is often quite good the morning after a big fall of spinner, when some of the previous night's spinner, utterly drowned and floating just under the surface, blow back into some spot and accumulate enough to attract a fish. The fly floats, or should be trimmed to float, *absolutely flush with the surface,* and for that reason is obviously unsuitable for use in open water when there is a good "lip" on the water, unless the light is very good or the angler has exceptional sight.

> HOOK. No. 9 long-shanked.
> WHISKS. Three cock pheasant tail fibres dyed purple, tied in flat, separated and varnished with clear Cellire ($1\frac{1}{2}$ inch).

BODY. Cream or white raffia with mauve waxed silk rib.

WING HACKLES. Two very large Andalusian or similar rusty brown cock hackles—with fibres about ¾ inch in length on each side of the stalk; i.e. 1½ inch overall.

TYING SILK. Black or chocolate.

The two hackles should be wound and fixed in the "spent" position and they should occupy ⅛ inch of the hook-shank. The fibres must be at absolute right-angles to the hook-shank, so that the fly floats flush with the water, held up by whisks and hackles.

DR. MICHAEL KENNEDY'S SEDGE FLIES AND PUPAE DRESSINGS

Murrough. (Sedge pupae).

BODY. Orange seal's fur mixed with a little hare's ear fur, with a slip of any darkish brown feather tied down on top of boddy as for "Green Peter."

RIB. Fine gold tinsel.

WING. Speckled hen wing quill.

LEGS. Mallard scapular fibres, with a turn of ginger hen hackle.

HOOK. 7–8 long shank.

Murrough. (Dry Fly). Sedge.

BODY. Green seal's fur.

RIB. Fine oval gold tinsel.

WING. Speckled greyish fibres from cock pheasant's wing, rolled and tied low over body.

HACKLE. Dark to medium natural red cocok, wound over wing roots.

Green Peter. (Sedge Pupae).

BODY. Green seal's fur with a slip of dark green olive feather fibres over the back, wound down on to body by ribbing.

RIB. Gold tinsel.

WING. Dark speckled fibres from pheasant wing. (To lie along sides in pupal position).

LEGS. Mallard scapular feather fibres or a few turns of ginger hen hackle.

HOOK. 9–10 Long shanked.

Green Peter. (Sedge Dry Fly).

BODY. Black seal's fur.

RIB. Fine oval gold tinsel.

WING. Dark speckled fibres from pheasant's wing.

BODY HACKLE. Coch-y-bonddu.

THROAT HACKLE. Coch-y-bonddu, wound over wing roots.

ALEC ILES "BREATHERLIZER"

Mr. Iles developed this fly specially for Chew Valley lake, and freely admits that it was of Canadian origin. It is supposed to represent the stickleback, and when seen actually in the water, it is as fair an imitation as one would want to see.

The fly must be fished fast, casting a long line and stripping as fast as one can—a long retrieve with one's left hand, holding the line on the rod handle with the right index finger. It is not necessary to fish the fly deep, but no doubt this would produce results if no fish were showing.

To obtain the best results, a "Worm Fly" should be used on the bob, either a "Silver Invicta" or a "Dunkeld" on the middle dropper, and the "Breatherlizer" on the tail *always*.

Included with the instructions Mr. Iles sent me was a photograph of seventeen fish taken at Chew Magna on 1st August 1960, 1 brown of 3 lb. 4 oz., the remainder rainbows ranging from 2½ lb. to 3 lb.

TAIL. Fibres from a soft black cock or hen's hackle.

BODY. Flat silver tinsel.

RIB. None.

WINGS. Two hot orange cock hackles, with two Green Highlander hackles outside, streamer style.

"EYES". Jungle cock tied close to head.

HACKLE. Badger. Wound as a collar.

HEAD. Black varnish.

HOOK. No. 6–8 down-eyed.

A. J. HAYTOR MIDGE PUPA DRESSINGS

Mr. Haytor gave the following four dressings in an article he wrote containing details of fishing at Sutton Bingham reservoir. I have used them myself on water far removed from Sutton Bingham, and can vouch for them from personal experience. I had two fish over two pounds in less than an hour, at Ham Bridge. Lake, the Piscatorial Society's water near Newbury.

The dressings are quite simple, but the underbody of silver is essential, and the thorax should be made large and round.

Black Pupa

HOOK. No. 12–14.
TYING SILK. Black.
UNDERBODY. Flat silver tinsel.
BODY. Black floss.
RIB. Silver wire.
THORAX. Black seal's fur.
HACKLE. Peacock herl with long "flue".

Brown Pupa

HOOK. No. 12–14.
TYING SILK. Brown.
UNDERBODY. Flat silver tinsel.
BODY. Brown (lightish) floss silk.
RIB. Gold wire.
THORAX. Orangy-brown seal's fur.
HACKLE. Orangy-brown ostrich herl.

Olive Pupa

HOOK. No. 16–13.
TYING SILK. Olive.
UNDERBODY. Flat silver tinsel.
BODY. Olive floss.
RIB. Gold wire.
THORAX. Olive seal's fur, with a little brown wool mixed in.
HACKLE. Olive ostrich herl.

Red Pupa

HOOK. No. 12–14.
TYING SILK. Scarlet.
UNDERBODY. Flat silver tinsel.
BODY. Scarlet floss.
RIB. Gold wire.
THORAX. Red and brown seal's fur mixed.
HACKLE. Brown ostrich herl.

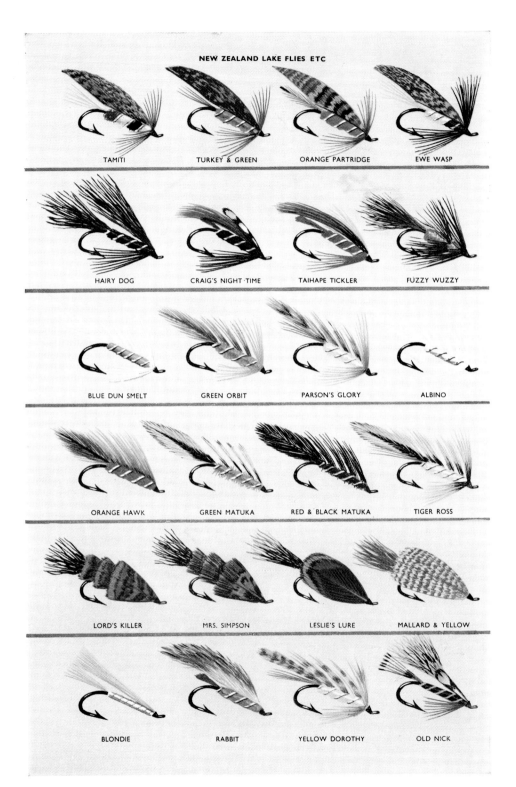

NEW ZEALAND LAKE FLIES

TERRY THOMAS SEDGE FLIES

No. 1. Standard

HOOK. No. 14–4 as required.
BODY. Fibres from a dark cock pheasant tail, wound as thickly as possible.
BODY HACKLE. Ginger cock.
WING. Grey deer body hair tied on flat with cut ends to the rear, and splayed out.
FRONT HACKLE. Ginger cock, wound over wing roots.

No. 2. Light Sedge

HOOK. No. 14–4 as required.
BODY. Fibres from a light cock pheasant tail wound on as thickly as possible.
BODY HACKLE. Ginger cock.
WING. Brown deer body hair tied on as No. 1.
FRONT HACKLE. Ginger cock.

No. 3. Dark Sedge

HOOK. No. 14–4 as required.
BODY. Black wool or chenille.
BODY HACKLE. Black cock.
WING. Black deer hair tied as for Nos. 1 and 2.
FRONT HACKLE. Black cock.

THE A. C. R. HOWMAN ("ALASTAIR ROSS") NYMPHS

This collection of dressings was one of the first selections I received for this new book, and were evolved by Major Howman by scouring round the weeds of his own lake and copying the insects he found. Major Howman is better known to you of course as "Alastair Ross", one of our most prolific contributors to the angling press, and he has contributed innumerable articles to such famous periodicals as *The Field*, *Trout & Salmon*, *Rod & Line*, and the *Fishing Gazette*.

I like particularly the simplicity of his dressings, and before giving them I do not doubt that some of the notes he sent me will be most useful:—

Corixa. "I found that the usual dressing was rather ineffective, and that a hackle doesn't really give the right impression. The dressing is made with hen pheasant tail feather with the butt end cut and shaped for the paddles and legs. The size attached (10) was best in April/May and a smaller one (12) in September."

Demoiselles. "These were most effective, and I caught trout throughout the season. I have some large and small nymphs in my aquarium at present, which confirms my view that the nymphs live, in some cases, more than a year. They vary a great deal in colour—green, through olive, to brown. June and July were the best months, and the dressings enclosed were the most effective. A nylon body did well too, but is difficult to taper. The wing cases and hackle are all from one feather tied butt end first."

Chironomids. "There are several of these and sometimes they appeared in vast numbers. The samples given were all effective, especially the little brown one (cock pheasant tail body), and the heron herl-bodied one. The latter was a very good evening fly and is, I think, rather like Oliver Kite's 'Imperial' which, when fished *in* the surface film and unoiled, was also a good fly. I found the 'Imperial' was best tied with a cream rather than a Honey Dun hackle. The pattern tied with a copper wire body and slate hackle was a 'killer' in May."

Alder Nymph. "I evolved this too late to do much good, but I hope to do well with it next season."

Sedge Pupa. "I watched two sedge pupa hatching one afternoon in August and dressed No. 11 as a result. It was an effective 'afternoon' fly and may well have been taken for a demoiselle in spite of having no tail!"

1. Pheasant Tail

HOOK. No. 12 or 13.

TAIL. Nil or chopped cock pheasant tail.

BODY. Cock pheasant tail, ribbed with brown silk.

WING CASES AND LEGS. Heron herl (Natural).

2. Chironomid I (A.R.)

HOOK. No. 12 or 13.

TAIL. Nil.

BODY. Copper wire ribbed black cotton.

LEGS. Slate hackle divided and clipped.

3. Chironomid II (A.R.)

HOOK. No. 12–14.

BODY. Cock pheasant tail.

LEGS. White ostrich herl.

4. Chironomid III (A.R)

HOOK. No. 12–14.

BODY. Natural heron herl ribbed slate silk.

LEGS AND THORAX. White ostrich herl.

5. Pond Olive (A.R.)

HOOK. No. 12–13.

TAIL. Clipped olive hackle.

BODY. Green nylon.

LEGS AND WING CASES. Green olive ostrich herl.

6. Pale Watery (A.R.)

HOOK. No. 12–14.

BODY. Grey nylon.

WING CASES AND LEGS. White ostrich herl.

7. Green Demoiselle (A.R.)

HOOK. No. 9–12 (or Mayfly), (10 is best).

TAIL. Clipped olive hackle.

BODY. Lovat wool (two-ply).

WING CASES AND LEGS. Green wool and olive hackle.

8. Brown Demoiselle (A.R.)

HOOK. No. 9–12. (10 is best).

TAIL. Ginger cock clipped.

BODY. Pale brown two-ply wool.

WING CASES AND LEGS. Brown wool and brown ginger hackle.

9. Olive Demoiselle (A.R.)

HOOK. No. 9–12.

TAIL. Grey squirrel (olive dyed) clipped $\frac{1}{8}$ inch.

BODY. Hare's fur (olive dyed), ribbed gold oval tinsel.

LEGS. Grey squirrel (other end to tail).

10. Corixa (A.R.)

HOOK. No. 10–12.

TAG. Silver tinsel.

BODY. White floss (fat) ribbed with silver.

WING CASES. Hen pheasant tail feather.

LEGS AND "PADDLES". Hen pheasant tail feather fibres cut to shape.

11. Green Sedge Pupa

HOOK. No. 10.

BODY. Olive floss, ribbed silver.

WING CASES. Blob olive seal's fur.

LEGS. Furnace cock (clipped).

HEAD. Orange silk.

12. Hatching Olive (A.R.)

HOOK.   No. 12.

BODY.   Hare's fur, ribbed gold oval tinsel.

TAIL.   Squirrel's tail (natural grey).

LEGS.   Squirrel's tail (natural grey).

13. Watershrimp (A.R.)

HOOK.   No. 12.

TAIL.   Olive hackle (round bend).

BODY.   Olive ostrich, ribbed silver.

OVER BODY.   Olive floss silk.

UNDER BODY.   Copper wire.

14. Alder Larva (A.R.)

HOOK.   No. 10–11.

UNDER BODY.   Copper wire.

OVER BODY.   White silk. Cream hackle clipped on top and underneath to ⅛-inch.   Silver tinsel.

HEAD.   Pale hare's fur.

15. Brown Beetle (A.R.)

HOOK.   No. 12–14.

BODY.   Peacock herl.

WING CASES (FULL LENGTH).   Golden Pheasant tail.

LEGS.   Golden pheasant tail clipped.

16. Stickleback (A.R.)

HOOK.   No. 9 (long Mayfly).

TAIL.   Olive hackle clipped to shape.

UNDER BODY.   Copper wire.

OVER BODY.   White floss well covered with silver tinsel.

FIN (DORSAL).   Olive hackle along back and clipped to shape.

FINS (VENTRAL).   Olive hackle, red hackle—mixed.

17. Chironomid IV (A.R.)

HOOK.   No. 12.

BODY.   Dark grey and green nylon.

LEGS AND THORAX.   Peacock herl.

18. Chironomid Pupa (A.R.)

HOOK.   No. 14.

BODY.   Knotted red double floss ¾-inch tied with red silk.

A SELECTION OF LAKE PATTERNS OF
NEW ZEALAND ORIGIN

There is no nonsense about New Zealand lake fly patterns, they were designed purely and simply to imitate the small fish on which this country's lake trout live and thrive. Although nymph and dry fly fishing is also popular on the lakes, it is the "long" flies which predominate.

The smelt is the prey of New Zealand lake trout, and it is the "Matuka" fly which is most used for its imitation. Actually the word "Matuka" is now the name of a whole series of patterns, and it originates from the bird of that name which supplied the earliest fly tyers with feathers for their lures. This unfortunately seriously reduced the number of Matukas in New Zealand but, in these wiser times when it is possible to get all the plumage we need from birds killed for the table (Turkey, Partridge, Grouse, Pheasant, Wildfowl, etc.), we have ample resources to cover the wide range of Matuka patterns without depleting the stocks of rarer birds.

The New Zealand Fly, although a "long" fly, has not so far made use of the long-shanked hook to any degree, but I think this is more due to tradition than any drawback a long-shanked hook may have. Extra length is imparted to the fly by extending the "wing" well beyond the bend of the hook, and in the main the construction of the flies is very simple indeed.

They consist usually of a fur, wool, chenille, or silk body, wound fairly thickly and an oval silver rib which has a dual purpose. It is used not only for making the fly more attractive or to protect the body, but also for binding down the "wing" on to the top of the hook shank. I think this needs a little more detailed description.

Two round-ended feathers such as the flank feathers from a hen pheasant are placed back to back, and the soft fibres stripped from the butt. A bottom section the same length as the body of the fly is drawn down at right angles to the stem, and the sides in contact with the body can also be stripped. The hackle stems are now bound down on top of the body, using the ribbing tinsel which is then tied in at the head in the usual manner. The upright hackle fibres are now stroked to the rear and the effect produced is shown in the drawings on page 150, and also in the coloured plate facing page 145. Incidently, the Hen Pheasant feathers are a very good imitation of the original "Matuka" feathers.

Another way this method of fly tying is used is in the "Turkey", "Grouse",

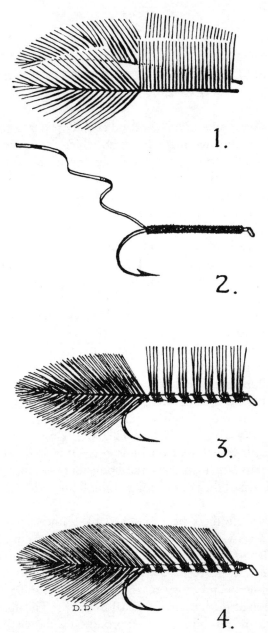

1.

2.

3.

4.

and "Partridge" series of flies. These take their name from the feather used
for the wing. To form these wings, a section of tail feather is cut, the length
of quill used being approximately the same length of the body of the fly. One

side is stripped off and the remainder tied in on top as the body in the same way as for the "Matuka", only in this instance the section of quill is bound down by the ribbing. The tail fibres are then stroked to the rear, and the result is a very durable long-winged fly with a lively water action. The usual term for these flies is "Split Partridge", "Split Turkey", etc. for reasons which are of course obvious.

Split Partridge

Jungle cock "eyes" are sometimes added to all these dressings, and the term for "Matukas" so tied is "Imperial".

The hair-winged flies used in New Zealand follow closely the same style as the North American Bucktails etc., with the exception, as I stated earlier, that in the main standard-length hooks are used.

I have not gone into detail over Australian lake flies, as these have a local interest only in my opinion. As yet the lakes there do not seem to have large stocks of smaller fish to make up a large proportion of the trout's diet, and the patterns which have emerged simulate the hornets, wasps, grasshoppers, and moths which abound on and around the waters of these lakes. Furthermore, as these insects bear little resemblance to those we would find around our own lakes, there does not seem much point in introducing them here, although some of their names may give some idea of the sort of fly which is used. I give them here merely as a matter of interest—"Smart's Hopper", "Hopper Hackle", "Ti-Tree Beetle", "Shannon Moth", "Bogong Moth", "Red Bug", etc., etc.

Albino

BODY. White chenille, floss, or wool.

RIB. Oval silver.

WING. Two white cock hackles, back to back, and tied down on top of hook with ribbing tinsel.

HACKLE. White cock, wound as a collar.

HEAD. Black varnish.

Awahou Special

TAIL. Cock pheasant rump fibres.

BODY. Red, yellow or green chenille.

RIB. Oval silver tinsel.

WING. Two pairs of cock pheasant rump feathers tied in to lie alongside body.

HEAD. Black varnish.

Black Phantom

TAIL. Black squirrel tail fibres.

BODY. Black chenille.

RIB. Oval silver tinsel.

WING. Six pairs of black pukeko feathers tied in to lie alongside body as in Mrs. Simpson. (Small dyed black heron feathers could be used as a substitute.)

HEAD. Black varnish.

Basket Moth

HOOK. No. 10–6.

BODY. Five or six alternate turns of yellow and black floss—fine.

HACKLE. Rather long-fibred speckled guinea fowl—about four turns.

(A good fly when moth are on the water.)

Black and Yellow (Devil)

TAIL. Black bucktail fibres.

BODY. Two equal parts of black and yellow mohair.

JOINT. Black cock hackle trimmed to about $\frac{1}{4}$ inch.

HEAD HACKLE. Black cock.

Blondie

TAIL. Bunch of white or cream mohair cut off flat, about $\frac{3}{4}$ inch long.

BODY. Flat silver tinsel.

WING. Another bunch of white mohair tied in at head and cut off level with end of tail.

A good example of a whitebait or smelt lure.

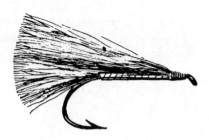

"Blondie." Smelt Imitation.

Blue Dun Smelt

BODY. Blue floss silk.

RIB. Oval silver tinsel.

WING. Two light blue dun cock hackles, back to back, and tied down on top of body with ribbing tinsel.

HACKLE. Light blue dun cock, wound as a collar, and fairly long in fibre.

HEAD. Black varnish.

Claret Jessie

TAIL. Claret hackle fibres.

BODY. Bronze peacock herl—tied thickly.

HACKLE. Claret cock or hen.

WING. Grouse tail.

Craig's Nighttime

TAIL. Red wool.

BODY. Black chenille.

RIB. Oval silver tinsel.

WING. Three blue pukeko feathers tied on to lie flat over body, plus a single jungle cock feather also tied on flat over the pukeko feathers. (Small heron feathers dyed blue could be used as a substitute for the pukeko.)

THROAT HACKLE. Black cock.

HEAD. Black varnish.

Dad's Favourite

TAIL. Red cock hackle fibres.

BODY. Red floss, seal's fur or chenille.

RIB. Gold wire.

HACKLE. Dark furnace.

WING. Starling, or grey duck in the larger sizes.

HOOK. No. 10–14.

Dorothy

(see "Yellow Dorothy".)

Ewe Wasp

TAIL. Yellow hackle fibres.

BODY. Yellow and black chenille.

RIB. Oval silver tinsel.

WING. Split speckled partridge tail.

THROAT HACKLE. Black cock.

HEAD. Black varnish.

Ewe Wasp (Barred)

TAIL. Yellow hackle fibres.

BODY. Alternate bands of black and yellow chenille.

RIB. Oval silver tinsel.

WING. Split grouse tail.

HACKLE. Black cock.

HEAD. Black varnish.

Ferris

BODY. Yellow mohair.

RIB. Oval gold tinsel.

WING. Two bright red cock hackles, back to back, and tied down on body by winding ribbing tinsel over hackle stem.

HEAD. Black varnish.

Fuzzy Wuzzy

TAIL. Black squirrel tail fibres.

BODY. Red, yellow, green, orange or black chenille.

RIB. None, but the body is divided in half by a black cock hackle.

HACKLE. Black cock, longer in fibre than centre hackle.

HEAD. Black varnish.

Golden Demon

TAIL. Ibis or substitute.

BODY. Flat gold tinsel.

RIB. Oval gold tinsel.

HACKLE. Bright orange.

WING. Brown mallard shoulder feather.

CHEEK. Jungle cock.

Gregg's Nighttime
(See Craig's "Nighttime")

Green Matuka

BODY. Green chenille, wool, or seal's fur.

RIB. Oval silver tinsel.

WING. Two badger hackles back to back, tied down on body by ribbing tinsel.

HEAD. Black varnish.

Green Orbit

BODY. Green chenille.

RIB. Oval silver tinsel.

WING. Two honey grizzle (cree) cock hackles dyed light olive or light green, and tied in "Matuka" style, i.e. on top of body with ribbing tinsel.

HACKLE. Light green, wound as a collar.

HEAD. Black varnish.

Grey Ghost (N.Z.)

TAIL. None.

BODY. Flat silver tinsel.

RIB. Oval silver tinsel.

WING. Two light grey cock hackles, bound down on to body by ribbing tinsel.

HEAD. Black varnish.

A light grey head hackle is sometimes added.

Hairy Dog

TAIL. Black squirrel tail fibres.

BODY. Any one of following colours: red, yellow, green, black chenille, or silver or gold tinsel.

RIB. Oval silver tinsel.

WING. Black squirrel tail fibres.

HACKLE. Black cock.

HEAD. Black varnish.

Ihi Green

TAG. Silver tinsel.

BODY. Green seal's fur or chenille.

RIB. Flat silver tinsel.

WING. Four black cock hackles, tied in as two pairs, back to back.

HACKLE. Black cock.

HEAD. Black varnish.

Ihi Red

Same as "Ihi Green" except for red body.

Invicta Jay

TAIL. Red ibis or substitute.

BODY. Yellow mohair or floss.

RIB. Oval gold tinsel-fine.

BODY HACKLE. Dyed yellow cock.

HEAD HACKLE. Blue jay, or natural black cock.

WING. From hen pheasant wing quill.

Jack Sprat

TAIL. None.

BODY. Flat silver tinsel.

RIB. Oval silver tinsel.

WING. Two badger hackles, back to back, and tied down on to body by ribbing tinsel.

HEAD. Black varnish.

A badger head hackle is sometimes added.

Jessie

BODY. Peacock herl—tied thickly.

HACKLE. Black or dark furnace cock.

WING. Brown mallard shoulder feather, tied low over body.

Leslie Lure

Sometimes called "Ohahau".

TAIL. Fibres from brown barred squirrel tail.

BODY. Red, yellow or green chenille.

RIB. Oval silver tinsel.

WING. Two pairs of hen pheasant wing front of body feathers, tied in to lie close alongside body.

HEAD. Black varnish.

Lord's Killer

TAIL. Black squirrel tail fibres.

BODY. Yellow, red, green, or orange chenille—any of these colours.

WING. Six pairs of woodcock breast feathers to lie alongside body.

HEAD. Black varnish.

An oval silver or gold rib is optional.

Mallard and Yellow

TAIL. Brown squirrel tail fibres.

BODY. Yellow chenille.

WING. Two pairs of grey mallard flank feathers tied in each side of body.

HEAD. Black varnish.

Bodies of orange, green, red, etc., can also be used.

Manuka Beetle

BODY. Light yellow floss.

WING CASE. Light green floss, tied in at tail, brought down over body and tied in at head.

HACKLE. Red game, underneath body only.

HEAD. Black silk—varnished.

Matukas

The variations of these dressings are too numerous for all to be included here. The grey, red, and green matukas, however, are illustrated, and the dressings given. They will give a good idea of the general appearance. Body colours can be varied, red, yellow, orange, etc., and the wings can be either of hackles tied back to back, or split tail feathers of partridge (most popular), grouse, or turkey, all tied in the same manner, i.e. with the solid stem of the hackle or the quill of the tail feathers tied down on top of the body with the ribbing tinsel. This method is illustrated in the dressings of "Parson's Glory", "Tiger Ross"(hackles), and "Tamiti", "Turkey and Green", "Orange Partridge", and "Ewe Wasp" (split tail feathers).

Jungle cock feathers, tied in close to head of fly, are sometimes added, and matukas tied with this addition are known as "Imperials".

Mrs Simpson

TAIL. Black squirrel tail fibres.

BODY. Yellow, red or green chenille.

WING. Six pairs of green cock pheasant rump feathers, tied alongside body.

HEAD. Black varnish.

Nimmo's Killer (Dry)

HOOK. No. 10–14.

TAIL. Three or four tippet fibres.

BODY. Half red, and half black, floss.

RIB. Fine flat silver.

HACKLE. Dark furnace. Two should be used if extra buoyancy is required.

Ohahau

(See "Leslie's Lure".)

Old Nick (1)

HOOK. No. 6–8.

TAIL. Golden pheasant tippet fibres.

BODY. Dark claret mohair or seal's fur.

RIB. Oval gold tinsel.

WING. Black-brown barred skunk or squirrel tail fibres.

HACKLE. Red game cock.

CHEEK. Jungle cock.

HEAD. Black varnish.

Old Nick (2)

TAIL. Ibis or substitute.

BODY. Red wool.

RIB. Oval gold tinsel.

HACKLE. Medium red.

WING. (Under) red goose or ibis. (Over) speckled partridge tail.

Orange Hawk

TAIL. None.

BODY. Orange chenille.

RIB. Oval silver tinsel.

WING. Two cream with brown centre hen hackles, back to back, and tied on "Matuka" style.

HEAD. Black varnish.

Orange Partridge

TAIL. Yellow hackle fibres.

BODY. Orange chenille.

RIB. Oval silver tinsel.

WING. Split partridge tail.

HACKLE. Red cock hackle, natural.

HEAD. Black varnish.

Another pattern where the body colours may be varied, i.e. "Yellow Partridge", "Green Partridge", etc.

Parson's Glory

TAIL. Orange hackle fibres.

BODY. Yellow chenille.

RIB. Oval silver tinsel.

WING. Two honey-grizzle (cree) cock hackles back to back, and tied down on top of body with ribbing tinsel.

HACKLE. Red game or cree, wound as a collar.

HEAD. Black varnish.

This is another pattern which can have variations of body colour.

Pukeko and Red

As "Taihape Tickler", but without the yellow hackle fibres.

Rabbit

TAIL. Reb wool.

BODY. Chenille—any colour from red, yellow, green, orange or black.

RIB Oval silver tinsel.

WING. A strip of skin from a rabbit's pelt, about $\frac{1}{8}$ inch wide and tied down in the same manner as "Matuka" wings, i.e. on top of body with ribbing tinsel.

HEAD. Black varnish, except for green-bodied fly, when red varnish is used.

Red and Black Matuka

BODY. Red chenille, or wool.

RIB. Oval gold tinsel.

WING. Two black hen hackles back to back, and tied down on top of body with ribbing tinsel.

HEAD. Black varnish.

Sam Slick

TAIL.   Tippet fibres.

BODY.   One third at tail of yellow floss, remainder of brown seal's fur.

RIB.   Oval gold tinsel.

HACKLE.   Brown partridge back feather.

WING.   Speckled partridge tail feather.

Split Turkey

TAIL.   Golden pheasant tippet fibres.

BODY.   Claret chenille.

RIB.   Oval gold tinsel.

WING.   Mottled brown turkey tail feather "split".   See below.

CHEEK.   Jungle cock.

HACKLE.   Wound in front of wings— claret.

HEAD.   Black varnish.

The instructions apertaining to the Matukas also apply to the Turkey series of patterns.   See "Turkey and Green" in illustrations.

Syd's Ginger

BODY.   Yellow mohair or floss.

RIB.   Oval gold tinsel.

HACKLE.   Four ginger cock hackles, tied on in the "Matuka" style.

HEAD.   Black varnish.

Taihape Tickler (Deadly Dick)

TAIL.   Red wool.

BODY.   Red chenille.

RIB.   Oval silver tinsel.

WING.   Three blue Pukeko feathers tied flat over body, with yellow cock hackle fibres over. (Small heron feathers dyed blue could be used as a substitute).

THROAT HACKLE.   Red cock.

HEAD.   Black varnish.

Tamiti

TAIL.   Yellow hackle fibres.

BODY.   In sections—red, yellow, black, yellow, chenille.

RIB.   Oval silver tinsel.

WING.   Split partridge tail.

THROAT HACKLE.   Natural red cock.

HEAD.   Black varnish.

Tamiti (Full dressing)

TAG.   Silver tinsel and red floss.

TAIL.   Golden pheasant crest.

BODY.   In sections as above, and each section butted with a natural red game hackle.

RIB.   None.

WING.   Strips of dark mottled turkey tail, tied in salmon-fly style, i.e. in strips without the quill.

THROAT HACKLE.   Natural red game cock hackle, tied under eye in salmon-fly style.

CHEEK.   Jungle cock.

HEAD.   Black varnish.

Taupo Tiger

BODY.   Yellow chenille or mohair.

RIB.   Oval gold tinsel.

WING.   Badger hackles tied in the "Matuka" style.

CHEEK.   Jungle cock.

HACKLE.   Badger, wound as a collar.

HEAD.   Red varnish.

Te Tauiwha

HOOK.   No. 1 long-shanked.

BODY.   Pale lemon chenille.

WING.   Pale grey mohair tied in at intervals along the body and extending beyond the bend of the hook.

HEAD HACKLE. Badger cock.

HEAD. Brown varnish.

Tiger Ross

TAIL. Orange hackle fibres.

BODY. Yellow chenille.

RIB. Oval silver tinsel.

WING. Badger hackles back to back, tied down on top of body, "Matuka" style.

HEAD. Red varnish.

This is another pattern where the body colour may be varied, also the tail colour, and on some patterns a badger hackle wound as a "collar" is also added. Jungle cock cheeks are also a popular addition to this pattern.

Tinopai

TAG. Round silver tinsel.

TAIL. Red ibis or substitute.

BODY. Two equal parts—of yellow and red mohair or chenille.

RIB. Oval gold tinsel.

HACKLE. Brown partridge back feather.

WING. Brown mottled turkey feather, with a strip of red goose over.

HEAD. Black varnish.

Turkey and Green

TAIL. Red game hackle fibres.

BODY. Green chenille.

RIB. Oval silver tinsel.

WING. "Split" turkey tail—brown mottled.

HACKLE. Red game, tied as a collar.

The wings of the "Turkey" series can also be tied in the orthodox salmon style, i.e. without the quill.

Turnip Fly

HOOK. No. 12–10.

TAIL. Fibres of black cock hackle.

BODY. Black thread, with crimson thread behind wings, approx. half and half of body for each colour.

WING. Grey mallard wing quill.

HACKLE. Black cock.

TYING SILK. Crimson.

Twilight Beauty (Dry)

TAIL. Fibres of natural medium red cock hackle.

BODY. Black tying silk.

WING. Starling wing feather.

HACKLE. Natural medium red cock hackle.

Waipahi—Red or Black

See "Red-bodied Waipahi".
"Waipahi Black", is the same, but with a black body.

Whitebait Flies

This is another series with multiple variations, some of which are listed in the Index. I refer to "Albino", "Blondie", and "Blue Dun Smelt", which are illustrated, and also "Te Tauiwha", "Dorothy", "Grey Ghost" and "Jack Sprat".

The following selection will no doubt also be useful to the tyer who wishes to build up a collection of this series.

No. 1

TAIL. White ostrich herl.

BODY. Flat silver tinsel.

WING. White mohair extending to end of tail.

HACKLE. White, tied underneath only, salmon fly style.

HEAD. Black varnish.

No. 2

BODY. Yellow mohair.

RIB. Flat gold tinsel.

WING. Badger hackles in any of the light colours, ranging from pure white to deep cream, and tied on "Matuka" style.

HEAD. Black varnish.

No. 3

TAIL. White and green mohair.

BODY. Flat silver tinsel.

WING. In three layers—white, green, white mohair.

HEAD. Black varnish.

No. 4

TAIL. Red mohair.

BODY. Flat gold tinsel.

WING. White or cream mohair.

HEAD. Brown varnish.

No. 5

BODY. Grey seal fur or wool.

RIB. Oval silver tinsel.

WING. Two grizzle (Plymouth Rock) cock hackles, tied on "Matuka" style.

THROAT. A short tuft of red wool.

HEAD. Black varnish.

No. 6

BODY. Flat silver tinsel.

RIB. Oval silver tinsel.

WING. Two grizzle cock hackles dyed orange, and tied on "Matuka" style.

HACKLE. Red cock, wound as a collar. (Dyed bright red.)

HEAD. Black varnish.

No 7

Same as No. 6, but with flat gold tinsel body, and oval gold rib.

No. 8

BODY. Orange floss silk.

RIB. Oval gold tinsel.

WING. Two badger cock hackles dyed bright yellow, and tied on "Matuka" style.

HACKLE. Dyed bright red cock, wound as a collar.

HEAD. Red varnish.

White Moth

BODY. White or yellow mohair.

RIB. Flat silver tinsel.

HACKLE. Light red cock, or white cock.

WING. White goose or duck strips.

HEAD. Black varnish.

William's Wonder

TAIL. Fibres from stiff natural red cock hackle.

BODY. Herl from a cock pheasant tail with a good red tinge.

WING. Tips of two brown cock hackles, set upright.

HACKLE. Natural brown.

HOOK. No. 14–18.

Yellow Dorothy

TAIL. Orange hackle fibres.

BODY. Yellow chenille.

RIB. Oval silver tinsel.

WING. Grizzle (Plymouth Rock) cock hackles, tied in the "Matuka" style, i.e. back to back, and tied down on top of body by the ribbing tinsel.

HEAD. Black varnish.

Alternative bodies: Red chenille, silver or gold tinsel.

A SELECTION OF STREAMER, BUCKTAIL AND
OTHER TYPES OF FLIES SUITABLE FOR
LAKES AND RESERVOIRS

Most of the patterns I give here are of foreign origin, but it has long been my theory that because of our changing pattern of still water fishing due to the introduction of the vast water conservancy schemes, flies of the type long popular in countries naturally blest with many expanses of open water should be just as successful here. I have proved this theory to my own satisfaction by taking a rainbow of 4 lbs. from Grafham on a "Black Matuka". As this fly resembles little less than a "Black Lure" with the tail hook broken off, I think my theory is justified even further.

It is never necessary to follow the dressing details slavishly, and any one of them can be varied to suit the personal ideas and requirements of the individual angler, another of the aspects which makes sense of tying one's own flies.

David Collyer, describing his "Red and Grey Matuka", confirms my theories concerning so called "foreign" flies, so I hope the following extensive list of dressings will contain patterns which will increase the "bags" of anglers in our waters.

The first section is culled from books of dressings, magazine articles, and personal contributors from North America, and I have made a careful point of selecting only those that have proved their worth over the years, or which have been specially recommended to me.

Why this type of fly should be so popular on the other side of the Atlantic and so relatively unknown, and therefore little used, by British anglers is hard to understand. Established British patterns have been known throughout the world for many years, so it would seem that although we have always been prepared to teach, there has been some tardiness in our ability to learn. This may in some way be due to the "mystique" once attributed to fly fishing, and also to fly tying, when a fly had to be a fly, even if one was trying to imitate a small fish. There can be little doubt that, to the North American fisherman, Streamer and Bucktail flies are an essential part of his kit, sometimes to the exclusion of conventional patterns as known and used by his British counterpart. (It might be as well at this juncture to define a "Bucktail" fly. The appellation is given to any hair-winged fly when its wings are roughly twice the length of a standard-length hook, and a pronounced "swimming" action thus imparted

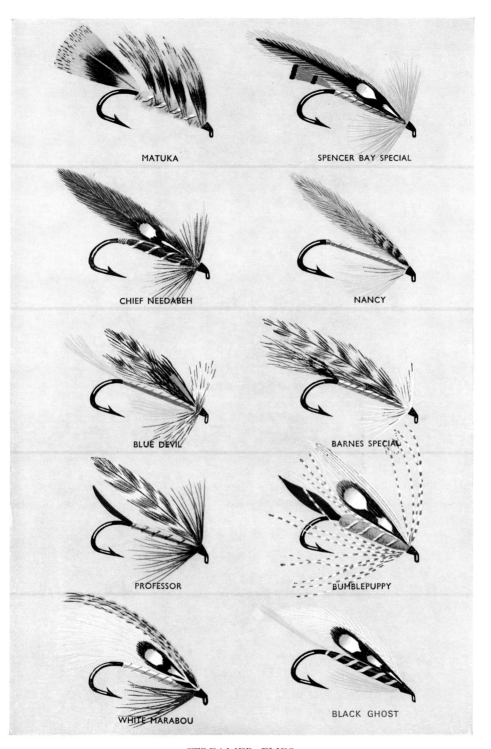

MATUKA

SPENCER BAY SPECIAL

CHIEF NEEDABEH

NANCY

BLUE DEVIL

BARNES SPECIAL

PROFESSOR

BUMBLEPUPPY

WHITE MARABOU

BLACK GHOST

STREAMER FLIES

Streamer Design.

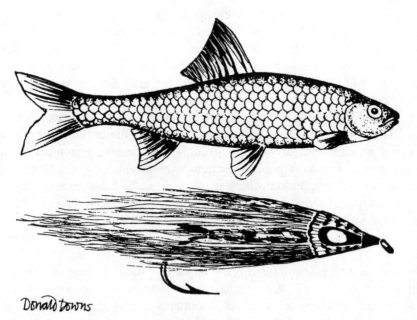

Donald Downs

Bucktail Design.

to the lure. Generally speaking, therefore, any hair-winged fly which produces a shape similar to that of a small fish when in the water may be regarded as a Bucktail Fly even though bucktail fibres may not have been used to form the wing.)

So, when you start to tie your Bucktails and Streamers, forget all about fly imitation and try to produce something which you think will look like another fish to the trout, and which has similar life and movement to a fish when it is being worked under the surface. One does not rely entirely upon the materials used for the effect, of course, and these lures once cast would not be retrieved in the same manner as a nymph, pupa, or larva. Each lure has to be fished in the manner most suited to the circumstances, be it an imitation of a small fish feeding unhurriedly on the bottom, or one in agitated flight from a predator on the surface.

If the "Polystickle" was the ultimate answer to small fish imitation, all these dressings would not be necessary, but as fortunately (for both us and the fish), this is not the case, I know that they will be of both profit (in terms of "bags") and interest to fly tyers, particularly in the attempts to produce something akin to nature's efforts and capable of fooling the quarry in its natural element. One factor may be more important than another, but as it is a recognised fact that game fish are usually highly selective, colour and size can be of as much importance as the speed at which the lure is retrieved and the depth at which it is fished. Furthermore, although some patterns given may seem a little gaudy, it should be remembered that some of the smaller species on which trout prey (even their own), can be very brightly coloured, and those that are small even when mature, are often much more brightly coloured during the spawning season. It should also be remembered that patterns which bear no resemblance to known species will also take fish, and this applies just as much to "long flies" as it does to more conventional types.

The "Sculpin" Muddler described on page 37 is an example of real imitation, yet the "Grey Ghost" Streamer given on page 166, and illustrated in the coloured plate, gives no indication of what its inventor was attempting to imitate. It is, however, one of the most popular patterns ever produced, and I think this is due to the overall impression which it gives of small fish representation, i.e. shape, dark top, light underside, flash, gill and fin suggestion, "eyes" of Jungle Cock, and the inclusion of materials which must give "life" to the lure when it is being fished—hackles, herls, and hair. It is what I would call a "when in doubt" fly.

Another point to be considered is the depth at which the lure will be fished, and also the time of day. When trout are fished for in big waters such as lakes and reservoirs, visibility is of major importance. Flies viewed under water lose brilliance because the relative loss of light tends to tone down all colours, particularly if the flies are fished deep. High visibility is more a matter of contrast so a black or dark-coloured fly when viewed from underneath by the fish, particularly in fading evening light, must have more visibility than one dressed in lighter tones. Bright colours fished near the surface are readily visible, but if one is fishing deep, contrasting colours such as black white etc., are much more visible than lighter colours of the prism. This is entirely due to the contrasting effect, and this should be borne in mind if one is in an inventive mood during fly tying.

The following dressings are examples of imitators—after that "you takes your pick".

Perch Fry

HOOK.   No. 4–6 long-shanked.

TAIL.   Reddy-brown cock hackle fibres cut to shape.

UNDERBODY.   Floss silk, fairly full.

BODY.   Gold Mylar piping marked with a brown felt pen to simulate bars. Alternative gold tinsel ribbed with wide brown floss silk.

WING.   Brown marabou feather fibres, with one or two orange ones over the top to form a crest.

THROAT.   Several white marabou feather plumes reaching about two-thirds the length of the body.

HEAD.   Black, with a yellow eye—black centred.

For Roach and Rudd—the Red Shiner

HOOK.   No. 2–6 long-shanked.

TAIL.   Red and white bucktail fibres mixed, fairly full.

BODY.   Flat or oval silver tinsel (wide) over a white floss silk underbody. Half way along body only. Now tie in a bunch of mixed red and orange bucktail fibres underneath and just long enough to cover the point of the hook. Cover half the remaining body with the silver tinsel and repeat the orange and red bucktail addition. More silver tinsel to the head of the fly and another bunch of bucktail fibres is added. The silver tinsel covers the butts of bucktail, and this method of body dressing is referred to as the Ozark style. Three or four bunches of bucktail can be used, according to the length of the fly.

WING.   White goat hair tied in directly above the hook, white bucktail next, followed by brown bucktail hair dyed slate blue (blue dun). All three sections of hair to reach as far as the tip of the tail.

THROAT.   This of course consists of the last tying of orange and red bucktail hair tied in under the body.

CHEEKS.　Amherst pheasant tippet feather tied in to represent gills.

"EYES".　Small jungle cock feathers tied close to head.

HEAD.　Grey silk varnished with clear varnish.

Minnow 1. (Bucktail)

HOOK.　No. 4–6 long-shanked.

BODY.　Embossed silver tinsel over white floss padding.

RIB.　Oval silver.

WING.　White bucktail extending beyond the bend of the hook to a distance about the same width of the gape.

SIDES.　A greenish-yellow hackle, with two light blue dun hackles each side. The sides to only be as long as the hook.

TOPPING OR OVERWING.　Peacock sword tail fibres.

"EYES".　Small jungle cock tied close to head.

HEAD.　Black varnish.

Minnow 2. (Streamer)

HOOK.　No. 4–6 long-shanked.

TYING SILK.　Black.

BODY.　Flat silver tinsel.

WING.　Two white saddle hackles, with one green saddle hackle each side, all to extend beyond hook.

TOPPING.　Several strands of Peacock Sword herl as long as the wings.

"EYES".　Jungle cock close to head.

HEAD.　Green varnish over the black tying silk.

Dace (Streamer)

HOOK.　No. 4–8 long-shanked.

TAIL.　Golden pheasant crest.

BODY.　White floss, slightly tapered.

RIBS.　Medium flat silver tinsel.

THROAT.　None.

WING.　Two light green hackles, outside of which are two blue dun hackles, one on each side. The wing should be half as long again as the hook.

CHEEKS.　Two small jungle cock feathers close to head.

HEAD.　Grey silk—varnished.

These few dressings should give you some idea of the theory behind streamer and bucktail flies and fishing, and should be considered in conjunction with the "Mylar" types on pages 30–33.

The following list gives the dressings of patterns which are considered "standards" overseas, not only in North America, but Australasia as well.

Careful study of the component parts, particularly as to colour, should give a very good idea of what the inventors of these flies were trying to imitate, and I hope that indulgence in this new aspect of fly tying will inspire sufficient interest for a collection of British Streamer and Bucktail flies to appear on the angling scene. I know this trend has already started (see the sections by Geoffrey Bucknall, Dick Walker, Dave Collyer etc., etc.), but the scope is so limitless that I also hope that it will be possible for me, in the not too distant future, to present a book on British Bucktail and Streamer flies, for use throughout the rest of the world as well as for home use.

Black Dog

TAIL. Black and yellow cock hackle fibres.

BODY. Black floss.

RIB. Oval silver.

THROAT. Short piece of yellow wing quill feather.

WING. Dun hackles—streamer style.

EYES. Jungle cock.

HACKLE. Black cock, wound as a collar.

HEAD. Black varnish.

Black Silver Tip

TAIL. None.

TAIL THIRD OF BODY. Flat silver tinsel

BODY. Black floss silk.

RIB. Oval silver tinsel, over floss only.

HACKLE. A few fibres of white cock hackle at throat.

WING. Black moose hair, or dyed bucktail.

Ken's Special

TAG. Gold tinsel.

BODY. Black floss silk.

RIB. Oval gold tinsel.

WING. White and orange bucktail.

Old Gold

TAIL. Golden pheasant topping.

BODY. Dark yellow wool.

RIB. Flat gold tinsel.

HACKLE. Furnace cock.

WING. Scarlet goose, covered by bronze mallard.

Joe's Hopper

TAIL. Scarlet hackle fibres.

BODY. Yellow ostrich herl.

BODY. HACKLE. Red game cock.

FRONT HACKLE. Grizzle cock dyed yellow, wound as a collar.

WING. Light brown speckled turkey wing quill.

Mickey Finn

BODY. Flat silver tinsel.

RIB. Oval silver tinsel.

WING. Scarlet and yellow bucktail, in three bands of colour, with red in centre. Upper yellow band is twice the size of lower.

Brook Trout

BODY. Rear two thirds—white floss, remainder pink floss.

RIB. Medium flat gold tinsel.

THROAT. First a bunch of hot orange hackle fibres, then a bunch of black hackle fibres, followed by a bunch of white hackle fibres.

WING. A small bunch of hot orange bucktail, over which is a pair of grizzle hackles dyed yellow, and outside of these a pair of olive green saddle hackles.

EYES. Jungle cock.

HEAD. Black varnish.

Brown Buffum

TAIL. Golden pheasant tippet fibres.

BODY. Orange floss.

RIB. Oval gold tinsel.

THROAT. Golden pheasant tippet fibres.

WING. Brown squirrel tail.

EYES. Jungle cock, tied close to head.

HEAD. Black varnish.

G.I. Joe

TAG. Silver tinsel.

TAIL. Fibres from scarlet wing quill feather.

BODY. Olive chenille.

HACKLE. Yellow.

WING. Two green olive cock hackles, back to back.

SHOULDERS. Strips from pintail flank feathers, two-thirds length of wing.

EYES. Jungle cock.

HEAD. Black varnish.

Golden Darter

TAIL. Section from mottled turkey wing quill.

BODY. Golden yellow floss.

RIB. Medium flat gold tinsel.

THROAT. Tip of jungle cock body feather.

WING. Two golden badger saddle or neck hackles.

EYES. Jungle cock.

HEAD. Black varnish.

Golden Pheasant

BODY. Yellow floss or chenille.

RIB. Oval silver tinsel.

WING. Two white cock hackles.

CHEEKS. Golden pheasant tippet feathers.

Green's Pot

BODY. Flat silver tinsel.

RIB. Oval silver tinsel.

WING. White and green bucktail, with a green hackle either side.

EYES. Jungle cock.

HEAD. Black varnish.

Gray Ghost (Plate facing p. 33)

BODY. Orange floss, thin.

RIB. Flat silver tinsel.

THROAT. Bunch of bronze peacock herl fibres, tied on directly under the head, then a bunch of white bucktail, both as long as the wing. Finally a bunch of yellow cock hackle fibres or a golden pheasant crest.

WING. Four medium blue dun cock hackles, tied streamer style.

CHEEKS. Silver pheasant body feathers, or barred widgeon throat feathers, wide.

"EYES". Jungle cock.

HEAD. Black varnish.

Marabou Special

TAIL. Tippet fibres.

BODY.   Flat silver tinsel.

RIB.   Oval silver tinsel.

WING.   White marabou plumes, with grey mallard flank feathers two-thirds of length.

SHOULDERS.   Golden pheasant tippets.

EYES.   Jungle cock.

HEAD.   Black varnish.

Mickey Finn

BODY.   Flat silver tinsel.

RIB.   Oval silver tinsel.

WING.   Yellow-scarlet-yellow bucktail.

EYES.   Jungle cock.

HEAD.   Black varnish.
(Tail of yellow and scarlet bucktail is optional).

Miramachi

TAIL.   Fibres from silver pheasant wing quill, and blue hackle fibres.

BODY.   Flat gold tinsel.

RIB.   Oval gold tinsel.

WING.   Blue and scarlet hackles, tied streamer style.

HACKLE.   Blue and scarlet mixed.

HEAD.   Black varnish

Cosseboom

TAIL.   Green floss silk.

BODY.   Green floss silk.

WING.   Grey squirrel tail.

HACKLE.   Green.

HOOK.   Long Shank.

TIP.   Flat silver tinsel.

Old Favourite

TAIL.   Short piece bright red wool.

BODY.   Flat silver tinsel.

HACKLE.   None.

WING.   Small bunch of white bucktail fibres, with a small bunch of brown ones over, and a few strands of peacock herl over all.

EYES.   Jungle cock.

HEAD.   Black varnish.

Racquette

TAIL.   Yellow cock hackle fibres.

BODY.   White floss, wound full, and tapered.

RIB.   Flat silver tinsel.

THROAT.   Small bunch of white bucktail as long as hook shank.

WING.   Yellow-black-yellow bucktail, with bunch of peacock herl over.

EYES.   Jungle cock.

HEAD.   Black varnish.

Ramsbottom's Favourite

TAIL.   Dyed red bucktail.

BODY.   Yellow seal fur.

RIB.   Oval gold tinsel.

HACKLE.   Coch-y-bondhu.

WING.   Bucktail dyed yellow, red, blue, green and brown.

HEAD.   Black varnish.

Shushan Postmaster

TAIL.   Section from mottled turkey wing quill.

BODY.   Yellow floss silk, full and tapered.

RIB.   Flat gold tinsel.

THROAT.   Section from red goose or duck quill (dyed).

WING.   Brown barred squirrel tail fibres.

EYES.   Jungle cock.

HEAD.   Black varnish.

Silver Darter

TAIL. Section from silver pheasant wing quill.

BODY. White floss, full and tapered.

RIB. Flat gold tinsel.

THROAT. Three or four pieces of peacock sword herl.

WING. Two white badger hackles.

EYES. Jungle cock.

HEAD. Black varnish.

Silver Sprat

TAG. Fine silver tinsel.

TAIL. Fibres of teal or mallard flank.

BUTT. Black ostrich herl.

BODY. Flat silver tinsel over a foundation of white floss.

RIB. Oval silver tinsel.

WING. A pair of dyed blue cock hackles back to back, with two grizzle hackles outside.

SIDES. Grey mallard flank.

EYES. Jungle cock.

HEAD. Black varnish.

Sneaky Joe

TAIL. Section from dyed scarlet wing quill feather.

BODY. Black chenille.

WING. Brown barred squirrel tail fibres.

EYES. Jungle cock.

HEAD. Black varnish.

Red Fin Streamer

TAIL. Red floss silk, or red marabou fibres.

BODY. Pink floss.

RIB. Flat gold tinsel.

THROAT. Exactly the same as tail, including size.

WING. Two black hackles back to back, with two golden badger hackles each side. All the same length, and extending beyond tail.

HEAD. Black varnish.

CHEEKS (optional). Two small jungle cock feathers, tied close to head.

Trout Perch

TAIL. Tip of a blue dun hackle.

BODY. White floss silk, wound full and tapered.

RIB. Flat silver tinsel.

THROAT. Blue dun hackle tip.

WING. Two or three strands of pink dyed ostrich herl, with a small bunch of brown squirrel tail, and a cree cock hackle each side.

EYES. Jungle cock.

HEAD. Black varnish.

Warden's Worry

TAIL. Scarlet wing quill, fairly long.

BODY. Yellow wool.

RIB. Oval silver tinsel.

HACKLE. Yellow.

WING. Brown bucktail.

HEAD. Black varnish.

Yellow Perch

TAIL. Fibres of yellow cock hackle.

BODY. White floss, wound full and tapered.

RIB. Flat gold tinsel.

THROAT. Tips of two orange cock hackles.

WING. Two well-marked grizzle saddle hackles, with two yellow hackles outside.

TOPPING. A few strands of peacock herl.

EYES.   Jungle cock.
HEAD.   Black varnish.

Yerxa

TAG.   Round silver tinsel.
BODY.   Yellow wool.
RIB.   Oval silver tinsel.
THROAT.   Yellow bucktail fibres.
WING.   White bucktail.
EYES.   Jungle cock.
HEAD.   Black varnish.

Blumarabou

BODY.   Flat silver tinsel.
RIB.   Oval silver tinsel.
WING.   Dyed blue marabou plumes, and two grizzle cock hackles.
EYES.   Short Jungle cock.
HEAD.   Black varnish.

General Ike

TAIL.   Fibres from a dyed scarlet duck or goose quill.
TAG.   Flat gold tinsel.
BODY.   Yellow chenille.
THROAT HACKLE.   Scarlet cock or hen's hackle.
WING.   Two Brown olive cock hackles back to back.
SHOULDERS.   Strips of widgeon flank feathers, two-thirds length of wing.
HEAD.   Black varnish.

Gold Sprat

TAG.   Fine oval gold tinsel.
TAIL.   Teal flank dyed yellow.
BODY.   Flat gold tinsel over a foundation of orange floss silk.
RIB.   Oval gold tinsel.
HACKLE.   Cree—honey grizzle.
WING.   A pair of deep yellow cock

hackles back to back, with two cree hackles outside.
SIDES.   Grey mallard flank dyed yellow.
EYES.   Jungle cock.
HEAD.   Red varnish.

Light Tiger

TAIL.   Fibres from silver pheasant body or wing feathers.
BODY.   Bronze peacock herl.
THROAT.   Fibres from dyed scarlet wing quill feather, tied in short.
WING.   Yellow bucktail.
EYES.   Jungle cock.
HEAD.   Yellow varnish.

Little Wonder

BODY.   Flat gold tinsel.
WING.   Grizzle hackles over scarlet—tied streamer style.
HACKLE.   Yellow.

Magog Smelt

BODY.   Embossed silver tinsel.
RIB.   Oval silver tinsel.
BELLY.   A few white bucktail fibres.
THROAT.   Two dyed red cock hackle tips.
WING.   First—yellow bucktail, second purple bucktail, with three or four strands of peacock herl as a topping.
HEAD.   Black varnish.

Cut Lips

TAIL.   Tip of a blue dun cock hackle.
BODY.   Pale lavender wool, tapering from shoulder to tail.
THROAT.   Tip of a blue dun hackle.
WING.   Two olive green saddle hackles on a small pattern (No. 8), four on any larger numbers.

EYES. Jungle cock.
HEAD. Black varnish.

Dwarf Sucker
TAIL. Fibres of light brown cock hackle.
BODY. Salmon pink floss.
RIB. Flat silver tinsel.
THROAT. Small bunch of white bucktail as long as hook-shank, and below this a small bunch of light-brown cock hackle fibres.
WING. Natural brown bucktail fibres, topped with a bunch of green peacock herl.
EYES. Jungle cock.
HEAD. Black varnish.

Fletcher's Super
TAIL. Scarlet duck wing quill.
BODY. Yellow chenille.
RIB. Oval silver.
WING. White and green bucktail fibres, with two blue cock hackles.
EYES. Jungle cock.
HACKLE. Yellow.
HEAD. Black varnish.

Blue Damsel
TAIL. Golden pheasant tippet.
BODY. Bronze peacock herl.
HACKLE. Blue cock tied as collar.
WING. Blue goose wing quill.

Black Demon
BODY. Flat gold tinsel.
HACKLE. Scarlet cock tied as collar.
WING. Black goose wing quill.

Ashdown green
TAIL. Two strips scarlet duck or goose quill.
BODY. Claret wool.
RIB. Flat gold tinsel.
HACKLE. Claret cock.
WING. White goose wing quill.

Jessabou
BODY. Flat silver tinsel.
WING. Natural brown hackles with peacock herl over.
EYES. Jungle cock.
HEAD. Black varnish.

Male Dace
BODY. White floss tapered and built up quite full at shoulder.
RIB. Flat gold tinsel.
THROAT. Tips of two hot orange hackles.
WING. Two olive green hackles with two golden badger hackles outside.
EYES. Jungle cock.
HEAD. Black varnish.

Alexandra Streamer
(A Canadian adaptation of our famous fly of the same name, which has outstanding success in its new habitat.)
TAIL. Fairly long section of dyed red goose or swan feather.
BODY. Embossed silver tinsel.
RIBS. Narrow oval silver tinsel.
THROAT HACKLE. A fairly wide black hackle, wound on as a collar and separated at the top to form the wing.
WING. A fairly large bunch of bright green peacock herl, extending beyond the tail of the fly. This should

be the long thin fronds taken from the "eye" section of a peacock tail, not the green sword herl used for the standard pattern.

Allie's Favourite Streamer

TAG.   Three or four turns of narrow silver tinsel.

TAIL.   None.

BODY.   Red floss dressed thin.

RIBS.   Narrow flat silver tinsel.

THROAT.   A sparse bunch of white bucktail extending beyond the bend of the hook, then under this a small bunch of orange hackle fibres under which is a small bunch of black hackle fibres both forming a short throat hackle.

WING.   Five or six strands of brigh, green peacock herl from the "eye" tail, as long as the rest of the wing over which are two orange hackles with a black hackle of the same length of these.   The wing should be as long as the bucktail, i.e. extending beyond the bend of the hook.

CHEEKS.   Jungle cock, fairly long.

HEAD.   Black varnish with a red band.

Anson Special Streamer

TAG.   Three or four turns of silver tinsel.

TAIL.   A small bunch of red hackle fibres.

BODY.   Peacock herl, not too fat.

RIBS.   Medium flat silver tinsel.

THROAT.   A few fibres of dyed red cock hackle, tied as a "false hackle" and with fibres as long as possible.

WING.   A thin bunch of white bucktail extending slightly beyond the tail.

SHOULDER.   The whole tip of a teal flank feather each side, approximately one-third as long as the wing.

CHEEKS.   Jungle cock, two-thirds as long as the shoulders.

HEAD.   Black varnish.

Atom Bomb (Yellow)

TAIL.   Tips of two bright yellow hackles, half the length of the hook.

BODY.   Silver Mylar tubular cord.

THROAT.   A small bunch of brown hackle fibres, rather long.

WING.   Bright yellow marabou plumes, over which is a small bunch of white bucktail, and over which are six strands of peacock herl, all extending to the tips of the tail.

HEAD.   Black varnish, white painted eye with red centre.

Atom Bomb (Grey)

Same as Yellow Atom Bomb, but with brown hackle tips for the tail, and grey marabou plumes instead of yellow.

Fraser Streamer

BUTT.   Two turns of dull orange chenille.

BODY.   Bright green wool, thick.

RIB.   Fine oval tinsel, silver.

WING.   Four white neck hackles.

SHOULDERS.   Short yellow neck hackle, extending two-thirds the length of wing.

CHEEKS.   Jungle cock.

HEAD.   Black varnish.

Barnes Special

TAIL. Jungle cock.
BODY. Flat silver tinsel.
HACKLE. White cock, tied full.
WINGS. Mixed red and white bucktail below, then two yellow hackles back to back with two grizzle hackles outside of these.
HEAD. Black varnish.

Red Badger

TAIL. Scarlet duck or goose quill.
BODY. Scarlet wool.
RIB. Flat gold tinsel.
HACKLE. Badger cock as collar.
WING. Two badger hackles back to back.

Titian

TAG. Orange floss.
BODY. Bronze peacock herl.
RIB. Orange floss.
HACKLE. Brown wound as collar.
WING. Fronds of bronze peacock herl with brown cock hackle each side, to be twice the length of body.

Grey Mare

TAIL. Scarlet duck or goose quill.
BODY. Flat silver tinsel.
RIB. Oval silver tinsel.
HACKLE. Brown cock.
WING. Two grizzle cock hackles back to back.

Red Abbey

TAIL. Scarlet goose or duck quill.
BODY. Scarlet floss.
RIB. Flat gold tinsel.

HACKLE. Brown cock.
WING. Brown bucktail.

Androscoggin

BODY. Claret floss.
RIB. Flat silver.
HACKLE. White bucktail tied underneath, and reaching to bend of hook.
WING. Two green hackles, back to back.
HEAD. Black varnish.

Professor

TAIL. Scarlet.
BODY. Yellow floss silk.
RIB. Flat gold tinsel.
HACKLE. Brown cock, wound as collar.
WINGS. Grizzle hackles.
HEAD. Black varnish.

Bumble Puppy

TAIL. Scarlet ibis.
BODY. White chenille.
RIB. Flat silver tinsel.
HACKLE. Grey mallard flank.
WINGS. White bucktail below, white goose or swan above.
SHOULDERS. Jungle cock.
HEAD. Black varnish.

White Marabou

BODY. Flat silver tinsel.
RIB. Round silver tinsel.
HACKLE. Scarlet cock.
WINGS. White marabou plume topped by several strands of green peacock herl.
SHOULDERS. Jungle cock.
HEAD. Black varnish.

Black Ghost

TAIL.   Golden pheasant crest.
BODY.   Black wool or floss.
RIB.   Flat silver tinsel.
HACKLE.   Golden pheasant crest.
WINGS.   White hackles.
SHOULDERS.   Jungle cock.
HEAD.   Black varnish.

Fingerling

TAIL.   Tip of scarlet cock hackle.
BODY.   Embossed gold tinsel.
HACKLE.   Red game cock.
WING.   Four golden pheasant tippets back to back to show three bars.
CHEEKS.   Scarlet goose wing quill with green peacock herl overall.

Red Phantom Streamer

TAIL.   Red hackle fibres.
BODY.   Bright red wool.
RIB.   Flat silver tinsel.
WINGS.   White marabou feathers.
HEAD.   Black head with white eye.

Sanborn Streamer

TAG.   Flat gold tinsel.
BODY.   Black silk, wound thick.
RIB.   Flat gold tinsel.
THROAT.   Bright yellow cock hackle.
WING.   Bright yellow neck hackles.
CHEEKS.   Jungle cock.
HEAD.   Black varnish.

Sanders Streamer

BODY.   Flat silver tinsel.
WINGS.   White bucktail, over which four grizzly saddle hackles.
CHEEKS.   Jungle cock.
HEAD.   Black varnish.

Greyhound Streamer

TAG.   Narrow flat silver tinsel.
TAIL.   Red hackle fibres.
BODY.   Red silk, thinly dressed.
RIB.   Flat silver tinsel.
THROAT.   Peacock herl, under which white bucktail, and under this red cock hackle.
WING.   Four grey saddle hackles.
SHOULDERS.   Jungle cock extending one-third the length of wing.
CHEEKS.   Jungle cock short.
HEAD.   Black varnish.

Green Drake Streamer

TAG.   Flat gold tinsel.
TAIL.   Black hackle fibres.
BUTT.   Peacock herl.
BODY.   Yellowish brown silk.
RIB.   Black silk.
THROAT.   Light brown cock hackle.
WING.   Two olive green saddle hackles, outside of which are two medium brown saddle hackles, one on each side.
CHEEKS.   Jungle cock, long.
HEAD.   Black varnish.

Jane Craig Streamer

BODY.   Flat silver tinsel.
THROAT.   White cock hackle.
WING.   Six white saddle hackles.
TOPPING.   Bright green peacock herl.
CHEEKS.   Jungle cock.
HEAD.   Black varnish.

Brown Ghost Streamer

TAG.   Flat silver tinsel.
BODY.   Dark brown silk.
RIB.   Narrow flat silver tinsel.

THROAT. Four or five strands peacock herl under which small bunch white bucktail, slightly longer than hook, beneath which golden pheasant crest feather curving upwards.

WING. Golden pheasant crest feather with four medium brown saddle hackles over.

SHOULDER. Teal body feather, dyed brown.

CHEEKS. Jungle cock.

HEAD. Black varnish.

Spencer Bay Special

TAIL. Fibres of golden pheasant tippets.

BODY. Flat silver tinsel.

HACKLE. Mixed, yellow and light blue cock.

WINGS. Two blue hackles back to back inside, and two furnace (red and black) hackles outside.

SHOULDERS. Jungle cock.

HEAD. Black varnish.

Chief Needabeh

TAG. Silver tinsel.

BODY. Scarlet floss.

RIB. Oval silver tinsel.

HACKLE. Mixed yellow and scarlet cock.

WINGS. Two yellow hackles back to back inside, and two orange hackles outside.

SHOULDERS. Jungle cock.

HEAD. Black varnish.

Nancy

TAG. Round silver tinsel.

BODY. Flat gold tinsel.

RIB. Oval silver tinsel.

HACKLE. Yellow cock.

WINGS. Two long green hackles back to back, with two shorter orange hackles outside.

CHEEKS. Any light brown mottled feather.

HEAD. Black varnish.

Blue Devil

TAIL. Golden pheasant crest.

BODY. Flat gold tinsel.

HACKLE. Grizzle cock, with golden pheasant crest feather under.

WINGS. Grizzle hackles, back to back.

CHEEKS. Blue peacock feathers, and blue kingfisher feathers.

HEAD. Black varnish.

Silver Minnow Bucktail

BODY. Medium flat silver tinsel, over fine wire.

RIB. Oval silver tinsel.

THROAT. Red cock hackle.

WING. White bucktail over grey squirrel tail hair.

TOPPING. Peacock herl.

HEAD. Red varnish.

Wesley Special Bucktail

TAIL. Golden pheasant tippet.

BODY. Flat silver tinsel.

RIB. Oval silver tinsel.

THROAT. Black cock hackle.

WING. White bucktail, over which blue-grey bucktail.

CHEEKS. Jungle cock.

HEAD. Black varnish.

Yellow Peril Streamer

BODY. Flat gold tinsel.

RIB. Oval gold tinsel.

THROAT. Yellow cock hackle.

WINGS. One red saddle hackle, between two grizzle saddle hackles.

CHEEKS. Jungle cock.

HEAD. Black varnish.

Brown Bomber Streamer

TAIL. Yellow hackle fibres.

BODY. Dark orange wool.

RIB. Narrow gold oval tinsel.

THROAT. Yellow bucktail.

HACKLE. Yellow cock.

WINGS. Four medium brown saddle hackles.

SHOULDERS. Yellow goose shoulder.

HEAD. Black varnish.

Binns Streamer

TAIL. A section of red and white goose shoulder feathers.

BODY. Medium flat silver tinsel.

RIB. Oval silver tinsel.

THROAT. Red and white saddle hackles tied as a collar.

WINGS. Two matched pairs, section of white goose married between two sections of yellow goose, all equal widths.

SHOULDERS. Gallena hen breast.

HEAD. Black varnish.

Colonel Bates Streamer

TAIL. Red duck shoulder feather.

BODY. Flat silver tinsel.

THROAT. Dark brown saddle hackle.

WING. Two yellow saddle hackles, with slightly shorter white saddle hackles each side.

SHOULDERS. Grey teal breast feathers.

CHEEKS. Jungle cock.

HEAD. Red varnish.

Dick's Killer Bucktail

TAG. Flat gold tinsel.

TAIL. Golden pheasant tippet rather long.

BODY. Peacock herl.

WING. Yellow bucktail.

TOPPING. A few strands from a wooduck or mandarin duck breast feather.

SHOULDER. Red turkey feathers.

CHEEKS. Jungle cock.

HEAD. Black varnish.

Dr. Burke Streamer

TAIL. Sword peacock fibres.

BODY. Medium flat silver tinsel.

RIB. Oval silver tinsel.

THROAT. Yellow cock hackle.

WING. Four white saddle hackles.

CHEEKS. Jungle cock.

HEAD. Black varnish.

Bucktail Fly with "Collar" Hackle.

ADDENDUM

SOME NEW PATTERNS

Ace of Spades
BODY.   Black seal's fur.
RIBBING.   Oval silver tinsel.
TAIL AND BACK.   Black hen hackle, tied Matuka style.
THROAT.   Guinea fowl hackle.
WING.   Brown mallard shoulder, to end of body.

Appetiser
BODY.   White chenille.
RIB.   Wide silver tinsel.
THROAT HACKLE.   Mixture of green and orange cock hackle whisks, and grey mallard drake fibres.
UNDERWING.   White turkey marabou.
OVERWING.   Grey squirrel tail.

Baby Doll

HOOK. No. 14–8.

TAIL. One of the pieces of white wool used for the body, cut short and teased out.

BODY. Two or three pieces of white wool (fluorescent if required), one of which is left at tail end while others are wound, and this is then brought down over the turns forming the body and tied in at head.

HEAD. Black silk.

Baddow Special

TAIL. Green D.F.M. wool or floss.

BODY. Bronze peacock herl.

RIB. Oval silver tinsel.

HACKLE. White cock.

HOOK. Long shank. (This is a version of the "Stick fly".)

B.W. (Barrie Welham) Nymph

HOOK. 12 down eye.

BODY. Brown wool—full.

RIB. Oval gold tinsel.

HEAD. White cock hackle tip cut short, and sloping backwards.

TAIL. 50/50 mixture of yellow and red D.F.M. filaments. *Short.* (Dyed fluorescent hackle fibres will also do.)

Black Beastie

HOOK. 4–8 long shank.

BODY. Black floss silk.

RIB. Flat silver tinsel.

HACKLE. Beard of hot orange marabou feather.

UNDERWING. Hot orange marabou feathers.

OVERWING. Black marabou feathers.

CHEEKS. Two silver pheasant flank feathers, one each side of hook.

HEAD. Fairly long, covered by a layer or two of fine lead wire.

Black Marabou Pupa

TAIL. A tuft of black marabou fibres.

BODY. Black floss.

RIB. Silver wire.

THORAX. Peacock herl.

BREATHING FILAMENTS. White hackle fibres.

Clarixa

FIRSTLY. Form hump of copper wire in the middle of the hook.

SECONDLY. At tail end tie in a length of brown raffia, white D.F.M. filament, silver lurex, and clear P.V.C. Cover the copper wire and rest of hook with the lurex, rib with the white D.F.M. filament, and then cover with the P.V.C. Bring down the brown raffia over the back, and tie in at head. Cover with several coats of clear varnish.

LEGS. Put a knot in each of two strands of cock pheasant centre tail fibres, and tie in to stretch along sides of fly.

HOOK SIZES. 8–14.

Collyer's Shrimp

TYING SILK. Olive or light brown.

BODY. Hair from a grey squirrel tail (spun onto tying silk).

RIB. Magenta fluorescent floss, or gold wire.

BACK. Olive goose, heron primary, or cock pheasant centre tail fibres.

Damsel Nymph (Taff Price)

HOOK.   8–10 long shank.

TYING SILK.   Yellow.

TAIL.   Olive hackle fibres.

BODY.   Seal's fur dyed olive, with a small amount of orange worked in.

RIB.   Yellow silk.

HACKLE.   Grey partridge dyed orange.

Dragon Fly Nymph (Taff Price)

HOOK.   8–10 long shank.

TYING SILK.   Black.

TAIL.   Two spikey goose quill fibres dyed olive.

BODY.   Mixed brown and olive wool, brown predominating.

RIB.   Yellow silk.

HACKLE.   Brown partridge.

HEAD.   Peacock herl.

Drone Fly

ABDOMEN.   Built up fat with yellow and black wool, or dyed goose fibres of same colours.

THORAX.   Black wool.

WINGS.   Blue Dun cock hackle points slanting back over body.

HACKLE.   Dyed yellow cock, rather sparse.

HEAD.   Crimson silk with one turn of dyed bright red ostrich herl.

Eyebrook Lure

TAIL.   None.

BODY.   Black floss silk.

RIB.   Oval silver tinsel.

HACKLE.   Black.

WINGS.   Badger hackles.

Glowstickle Fore and Aft

BODY.   Luminous plastic strip wound over a white floss underbody. Cigar shape.

HACKLES.   (Fore and aft.) Long white or buff cock hackles.

Grafham Grey

HOOKS.   Two in tandem—nickel plated.

BODY.   Dark grey wool.

RIB.   Oval silver tinsel.

TAIL.   Golden pheasant crest.

WING.   Two badge cock hackles tied over body.

HACKLE.   Badger (soft) wound as a collar.

Hanningfield Lure

TAIL.   Orange cock hackle fibres.

BODY.   White wool (fluorescent if so desired).

RIB.   Oval silver tinsel.

WING.   White goat hair with a strip of brown mottled turkey fibres over.

HACKLE.   (Two.) First a short blue hackle, followed by a hot orange hackle.

HEAD.   Black.

Leprechaun

TAIL.   Lime D.F.M. cock hackle fibres.

BODY.   D.F.M. lime chenille.

RIB.   Oval silver tinsel.

THROAT HACKLE.   Lime green cock hackle.

WINGS.   Two pairs of D.F.M. lime green cock hackles.

Longhorns (Sedge Pupae)

HOOK. No. 12–10.

BODY. Abdomen and thorax—ostrich herl.

HORNS. Two strands of cock pheasant tail tied in to slant back over body, and twice its length.

HACKLE. Brown partridge (in all cases).

COLOUR COMBINATIONS

1. Sea green abdomen—sepia thorax.
2. Sea green abdomen—light chestnut thorax.
3. Amber abdomen—light chestnut thorax.

Marabou Bloodworm Larva

TAIL. A tuft of red marabou feathers.

BODY. Red floss.

RIB. Silver wire.

THORAX. Peacock herl.

BREATHING FILAMENTS. White hackle fibres.

HOOK. 14 long shank.

Masso's Vulture

HOOK. No. 6 d/e.

BODY. The tying silk coated with pearl nail varnish.

UNDERWING. Brown squirrel tail fibres. (Wallaby fur in the original.)

SIDE WINGS. Black hen hackles.

CHEEKS. Jungle cock substitute.

HEAD. Black varnish. (A good "bird-like" head.)

EYES. White varnish with black varnish centres.

Master Cutler

BODY. Silver Sellotape, folded over hook shank, and cut to fish shape.

HACKLE. Hot orange cock hackle.

WING. Black squirrel tail.

Missionary

TAIL. White cock hackle fibres.

BODY. White wool, pulled and spun on.

WING. A few fibres of black turkey tail feather, with strips of dark teal on each side. Extending well beyond bend of hook.

HACKLE. White cock.

Monday's Child

HOOK. 10–14.

TAIL. Dyed scarlet marabou herl, or soft flute from base of a dyed red goose or swan shoulder feather.

BODY. Orange seal fur, on orange silk. Fairly plump.

RIB. Oval silver tinsel.

HACKLE. Four or five turns of a large soft white cock hackle, or hen's hackle, sloping backwards. A successful fly by Mike Sabine, secretary of the Fly Dressers Guild. He also recommends an underbody of silver lurex.

Nailer

TAIL. Scarlet cock hackle fibres.

BODY. Flat gold tinsel.

RIB. Oval gold tinsel.

WINGS. Four scarlet cock hackles, with brown mottled turkey tail strips over.

HACKLE. Four turns of natural medium cock hackle, wound as a collar. (Can be tied as a tandem also.)

Olive Sun Nymph

HOOK. No. 12–14.

BODY. Greenish yellow fluorescent floss, slim.

RIB. Fine gold oval tinsel.

HEAD. A few turns of peacock herl.

TAIL. A golden pheasant crest as long as the body.

Ombudsman

Wrap hook shank with a layer of copper wire to weight it.

BODY. Bronze peacock herl.

RIB. Black silk, or copper wire.

WING. Sloping backward from eye, and forming an almost tubular shape over the first two-thirds of hook, ending with a point well beyond bend of hook. Use any mottled wing feather.

HACKLE. Softish brown cock, wound as a "collar".

Persuader

TYING SILK. Orange.

BODY. Five strands of white ostrich, trimmed close.

RIB. Round silver tinsel.

THORAX. Orange seal fur. Wing cases, strands of dark brown turkey.

Plastazote Corixa

HOOK. No. 12–14.

BODY. A piece of Plastazote cut to corixa shape, which is slit and glued over hook.

BACK. Brown feather fibres tied in at tail, taken over back and tied down at head.

OARS. Two cock pheasant tail fibres tied in at head and sloping back over body, beyond bend of hook.

Rasputin

HOOK. 10–8 long shanked.

BODY. A piece of Plastazote cut to minnow shape.

Back and "hackle". A fairly wide piece of brown speckled turkey fibres, tied in at tail and taken over back, the ends being split into two equal parts and tied to stick out each side. Trim to about ⅓ length of body.

HEAD. Brown silk.

Rat Tailed Maggot

HOOK. No. 12.

TAILS. Two long fibres of undyed swan or goose.

BODY. White fluorescent wool.

RIB. Stripped ginger cock's hackle stalk.

Rusty Squirrel

TAIL. Squirrel tail dyed black.

BODY. First weight with fuse or lead wire, then cover with oval silver tinsel.

HACKLE. Hot orange.

WING. Brown squirrel tail.

COLLAR. D.F.M. chenille.

EYES. Chrome bead chain, small or medium.

Spuddler

HOOK. 10–6 long shanked.

TAIL. A bunch of brown calf tail fibres.

BODY. Cream wool, with a few turns of fine fluorescent wool at the throat.

WING. Four long Cree cock hackles tied in two pairs with fibres of brown squirrel hair tied over the top. The wings are tied in flat.

HEAD. As for Muddler minnow, but cut shorter on the underside.

Squire mallard

TAIL. Tippet fibres.

BODY. Tail half white lurex, second half gold lurex, both ribbed with gold wire.

HACKLE. Orange hen.

WING. Brown mallard.

Tornado

HOOK. 8–6 long shanked.

BODY. White floss silk.

RIB. Oval silver tinsel.

THROAT. Orange cock hackle.

WINGS. In three layers. Underwing of white bucktail, middle wing of pale blue goat hair, top wing of black bucktail.

Whisky

HOOK. Long shank.

BODY. Medium gold tinsel wound over a scarlet floss body, which should show as a rib.

HACKLE. Hot orange.

WING. Hot orange calf tail hair, or hot orange hackles.

White Lure

TAIL. White hackle fibres.

BODY. White wool.

RIB. Oval silver tinsel.

HACKLE. White cock.

WINGS. Four white cock hackles.

INDEX

Patterns in **bold type** are illustrated in colour